PLANNING USES AND USE CLASSES

PLANNING USES AND USE CLASSES

Michael Redman

SOLICITOR WITH CLIFFORD CHANCE

1989

THE ESTATES GAZETTE LIMITED

151 WARDOUR STREET, LONDON W1V 4BN

First published 1989
ISBN 0 7282 0129 1

*This book was commissioned
and produced for the Estates Gazette Limited
by Leaf Coppin Publishing Ltd*

Author's Note
So far as possible the law
is as stated on 1 May 1989

Phototypeset by Input Typesetting, London
Printed by Hobbs the Printers of Southampton SO9 2UZ

CONTENTS

TABLE OF CASES

1 REGULATING USES

The planning system regulates operational development and development involving a material change of use. Development means the carrying out of building, engineering, mining or other operations in, on, over or under land, or the making of a material change in the use of any buildings or other land.[1] This definition of development is the corner-stone of planning law as planning permission is needed to carry out development.

It will be seen that the planning system regulates the use to which a person may put his land and buildings as well as the operations which can take place on his land. This has enormous implications. The width of the definition means that the local planning authority can control a business use within a house, a retail use within a warehouse, a building society use in a high street shop, an industrial use within a domestic garage and many other such uses within buildings or on land which have not previously been used for those purposes.

However it is not every change of use which requires planning permission, otherwise the local planning authority would be faced with a barrage of applications for planning permission to change the use of a butcher's shop, say, to a grocer's shop. The legislation restricts the changes of use requiring planning permission in three ways. The first is to provide that only a *material* change of use requires planning permission.

In this respect the change of use must be material from a planning point of view. In assessing whether the change is material, one is justified in distinguishing between the character of the uses and asking if they are different.[2] Changes in the identity of the occupant[3] and changes which are *de minimis*[4] will not usually be regarded as material.

The second way of restricting the need to obtain planning permission is by providing that in the case of buildings or other land which are used for a purpose specified in any Use Class, no development occurs if the buildings or other land are used for any other purpose of the same Use Class.[5] Various uses are grouped together into a number of Uses Classes so that changes of use within a particular Use Class do not constitute development. In the example given above, the butcher could convert his shop into a greengrocer's because the change would not be considered material and, in any event, the change would be covered by the Shops Class of the Use Classes Order.[6]

The third way is to grant planning permission by means of development orders to obviate the need for a specific planning application. The General Development Order[7] grants planning permission for various forms of development including some changes of use between Use Classes.

The General Development Order is of general application. Planning permission may be granted by Special Development Order for particular development in defined areas. Some areas enjoy a wide planning permission granted under an Enterprise Zone Scheme or Simplified Planning Zone Scheme.[8]

Use Classes Order

A new Use Classes Order was issued in 1987. The Government saw the new Use Classes Order as 'a means of deregulation',[9] to simplify the planning system and reduce the burden of control. An efficient and simple system is said to speed the planning process and facilitate much needed development which helps to create jobs – in construction, in commerce and industry and in small firms.[10] The old Use Classes Order had not been substantially changed since it was first introduced in 1948, and it was in need of review in the light of modern conditions. The new Use Classes Order had to take account of the requirements of 'high-tech' firms where manufacturing, offices, research and development, warehousing and other activities may be carried on in a single building and where the mix of uses and space utilisation may need to be constantly changed and adapted to the needs of business. Since the Use Classes Order was intended to permit and not restrict compatible uses, it was essential that it should be designed to do this effectively.[11] To this end, the new Use Classes Order was introduced.

Need for Planning Permission

It may be necessary to apply for planning permission to introduce a new use on to land. Planning permission is required to carry out development[12] which includes making a material change in the use of any buildings or other land.[13] An application for planning permission should be made to the local planning authority who will generally be the district council in a non-metropolitan county, the council of a metropolitan district or the council of a London borough.[14] In dealing with the application, the local planning authority must have regard to the provisions of the development plan and to any other material considerations. They may grant the application either unconditionally or subject to such conditions as they think fit or they may refuse the application.[15]

Development Plans

In deciding whether to grant planning permission for a material change of use, the development plans must be considered. The development plans consist of the structure plan[16] which deals with the area of the county and the local plan which deals with the whole or part of the district.[17] In London and metropolitan districts, the two-tier plans are being phased out in favour of unitary development plans.[18] For the rest of the country, the Government is to introduce legislation replacing structure plans with statements of county policies and replacing local plans with district development plans.[19] These development plans contain policies which must be considered by the local planning authority when they decide whether or not planning permission should be granted.

However, local planning authorities should not slavishly follow the development plan when considering planning applications. Circular 14/85, Development and Employment, points out that development plans are only one of the material considerations that must be taken into account when dealing with planning applications.

> Many development plans were approved several years ago, often several years after they had been prepared and based on even earlier information. The policies which they contain, and the assumptions on which they were based, may therefore be out of date and not well related to today's conditions. They cannot be adapted rapidly to changing conditions, and they cannot be expected to anticipate every need or opportunity for economic development that may arise. They should not be regarded as overriding other material considerations, especially where the plan does not deal adequately with new types of development or is no longer relevant to today's needs and conditions – particularly the need to encourage employment and to provide the right conditions for economic growth.[20]

Government Policies

In addition to development plans, the local planning authority must have regard to other material considerations.[21] Important amongst the material considerations are those of government policies as expressed in White Papers, circulars and Planning Policy Guidance Notes ('PPGs'). These statements of policy are important when a local planning authority has to decide whether to grant an application for planning permission for a material change of use.

Since 1980 there have been a succession of White Papers and circulars dealing with the need to encourage business and employment. In 1980, local planning authorities were enjoined 'to adopt a more positive attitude to planning applications; to facilitate development; and always to grant planning permission, having regard to all material considerations, unless there are sound and clear-cut reasons for refusal'. This advice was contained in Circular 22/80, Development Control Policy and Practice, which aimed to secure a general speeding up of the system and to ensure that development was only prevented or restricted where this served a clear planning purpose and the economic effects had been taken into account. The Government expressed itself particularly keen to encourage the formation and expansion of small-scale businesses.[22] It went on to support the setting up of small-scale businesses in redundant buildings such as disused agricultural buildings, industrial, warehouse or commercial premises:

> The fact that an activity is a non-conforming use is not a sufficient reason in itself for refusing planning permission or taking enforcement action. It substantially eases the problems of starting and maintaining small-scale businesses if permission can be given for such uses to be established in redundant buildings such as disused agricultural buildings, industrial, warehouse, or commercial premises, on derelict sites or in unsuitable housing. It may be helpful where planning authorities are able to use information already available to them to identify in advance disused buildings in their own area suitable for the location of such small-scale businesses. Therefore when small-scale commercial and industrial activities are proposed particularly in existing buildings, in areas which are primarily residential or rural, permission should be granted unless there are specific and convincing objections such as intrusion into open countryside, noise, smell, safety, health or excessive traffic generation. Where there are planning objections it will often be possible to meet them to a sufficient degree by attaching conditions to the permission or by the use of agreements under section 52 of the Town and Country Planning Act 1971 rather than refusing the application. Such opportunities should be taken.[23]

In 1984, Circular 16/84, Industrial Development, was issued. It stated that industrial development was vital if economic recovery was to be sustained. It points out that light industry and many forms of small business can be accommodated in residential areas without creating unacceptable traffic, noise or other adverse effects and without detriment to the amenity of the area as reflected in the definitions of the Use Classes Order. It goes on:

> Local residents may be worried at the prospect of such industrial, or indeed any form of development, and may need particular reassurance and explanation, but it may often be possible to frame conditions which will enable planning permission to be given and make the development more acceptable to them. At the same time, all authorities will recognise that the prospects for bringing into use vacant buildings and sites in any area could be jeopardised if unrealistic and rigid restrictions are imposed – or maintained – on types of development acceptable or if unnecessary conditions restrict the way in which the permission can be used.[24]

In the next year, 1985, Circular 14/85, Development and Employment, stressed that new development contributed to economic activity and the provision of jobs. It was in the national interest to encourage it. It pointed out that development proposals were not always acceptable. There were other important objectives to which the Government was firmly committed: the need to preserve our heritage, to improve the quality of the environment, to protect the green belts and conserve good agricultural land. However, it went on to say that the planning system failed in its function whenever it prevented, inhibited or delayed development which could reasonably have been permitted: 'There is therefore always a presumption in favour of allowing applications for development having regard to all material considerations, unless that development would cause demonstrable harm to interests of acknowledged importance.'[25]

Following Circular 14/85, Circular 2/86, Development by Small Businesses, stated that small firms were one of the country's greatest resources in the expansion of the economy and employment and that local planning authorities could do a great deal to guide small firms through the requirements of the planning system. It restated that many new uses could be introduced without harm into rural areas or settlements, particularly in existing buildings:

> In such cases, permission should be granted unless there are specific and convincing objections that could not satisfactorily be overcome by imposing conditions. It is important that wherever possible redundant agricultural buildings should be freed for use by other industries to bring them back into use and to diversify the rural economy. Local authorities should bear in mind that many commercial or light industrial uses create less noise nuisance than some activities related to agriculture.[26]

In January 1988 the Planning Policy Guidance Note on Industrial and Commercial Development and Small Firms stressed that light industry, offices and many forms of small businesses can generally be accommodated within residential areas without creating unacceptable increases in traffic, noise or other adverse effects. The fact that an activity is a nonconforming use is not sufficient reason in itself for refusing planning permission or taking enforcement action:

> When small-scale commercial and industrial activities are proposed, particularly in existing buildings, in areas which are primarily residential or rural, permission should be granted unless there are specific and convincing objections such as intrusion into open countryside, noise, smell, safety, health or excessive traffic generation. Where there are such planning objections, attempts should be made to meet them

by specific conditions attached to the grant of permission rather than refusing permission.[27]

Redundant Buildings

Government policy is to ensure that redundant rural buildings can be used to reduce demands for new development while also helping new enterprises and providing new jobs:

> Existing circulars already emphasise the fact that many commercial and other activities can be carried on in rural areas without causing unacceptable disturbance and that proposals for the re-use of redundant buildings should not be refused unless there are specific and convincing reasons which cannot be overcome by attaching reasonable conditions to the planning permission. The Government has made it clear that these principles apply to the re-use of redundant buildings in Areas of Outstanding Natural Beauty and Green Belts as well as elsewhere in the countryside.[28]

This policy is important in respect to listed buildings. Circular 8/87, Historic Buildings and Conservation Areas – Policy and Procedures, gives specific advice for farming and rural buildings:

> Changing patterns of farming and rural life also mean that new uses must be found for buildings such as stables, coach houses, barns, and oast houses that play such an important part in the history and appearance of the countryside. All possible solutions should be explored. If these buildings are used as workshops, craft studios or as holiday accommodation, they can often make a contribution to the rural economy by providing employment.[29]

The circular acknowledges that 'new uses for old buildings may be the key to their preservation.' While the best use for an historic building is obviously the use for which it was designed, it accepts that in many cases the continuation of the original use is not now a practicable proposition and it will often be essential to find appropriate alternative uses:[30]

> Local authorities should therefore be flexible in dealing with planning applications for changes of use of buildings of architectural or historic interest or other applications for consent for works associated with a change of use. It is suggested that they should, wherever possible, make a survey of such buildings in their area and make a provisional assessment of the types of new uses which they would be prepared to accept. This is particularly important when the buildings are empty,

either in their entirety or on the upper floors. With this information available, authorities should be able to respond more quickly when applications for a change of use are submitted.[31]

Appeals

If planning permission is refused or granted subject to conditions, the applicant has a right of appeal to the Secretary of State for the Environment.[32] He also has a right of appeal against non-determination of his application within the designated two-month period. The Secretary of State may allow or dismiss the appeal, or may reverse or vary any part of the decision of the local planning authority, whether the appeal relates to that part or not and may deal with the application as if it had been made to him in the first instance.[33]

An appeal is dealt with by way of public inquiry, hearing or by written representations. The decision is usually delegated to an inspector appointed by the Secretary of State[34] although in important cases the Secretary of State himself will make the decision. In addition to determining appeals the Secretary of State can call in an application made to the local planning authority for his own determination.[35] He will only call in applications if planning issues of more than local importance are involved.[36]

In determining an application or appeal, the Secretary of State must have regard to the development plan and any other material considerations. An application may be made to the High Court to quash a decision of the Secretary of State on the grounds that it was invalid owing to its having been made outside his powers or to the relevant requirements not having been complied with.[37]

Enforcement Action

The local planning authority may take enforcement action against uses which have been carried out without planning permission. The change of use must have occurred since the end of 1963 or in the case of a change of use of any building to use as a single dwelling-house not more than four years previously. If the local authority considers it expedient to do so, having regard to the provisions of the development plan or other material considerations, it may issue an enforcement notice requiring the breach of planning control to be remedied. The enforcement notice should specify any matters alleged to constitute a breach of planning control, any steps required to remedy the breach and steps for the purpose of complying with any planning permission or of removing or alleviating any injury to amenity caused by the development.[38]

A person having an interest in land to which an enforcement notice relates, may, at any time before the date specified in the notice as the date on which it is to take effect, appeal to the Secretary of State against the enforcement notice.[39] The date on which the enforcement notice is to take effect should be not earlier than twenty-eight days after service of the enforcement notice.[40] It should be noted that the time limits for appeal are strict and will not be extended. The notice of appeal must be in writing and reach the relevant office of the Department of the Environment before the date specified in the notice.[41] Where an appeal is brought, the enforcement notice has no effect pending the final determination or withdrawal of the appeal.[42] This has now been interpreted to include the period taken to dispose of an appeal to the High Court against the Secretary of State's decision.[43]

There are several grounds on which an appeal may be made to the Secretary of State.[44] These are:

(a) that planning permission ought to be granted for the development to which the notice relates or, as the case may be, that a condition or limitation alleged in the enforcement notice not to have been complied with ought to be discharged;

(b) that the matters alleged in the notice do not constitute a breach of planning control;

(c) that the breach of planning control alleged in the notice has not taken place;

(d) that, in the case of certain development, the four-year period from the date of the breach of planning control had elapsed at the date when the enforcement notice was issued. Development falling within the four-year rule includes operational development, the making without planning permission of a change of use of any building to use as a single dwelling-house and failure to comply with a condition which prohibits or has the effect of preventing a change of use of a building to use as a single dwelling-house.[45]

(e) in the case of other notices, that the breach of planning control alleged by the notice occurred before the beginning of 1964;

(f) that copies of the enforcement notice were not served as required;

(g) that the steps required by the notice to be taken exceed what is necessary to remedy any breach of planning control or to achieve a purpose of making the development comply with the terms of any planning permission or of removing or alleviating any injury to amenity which has been caused by the development.

(h) that the period specified in the notice as the period within which any step is to be taken falls short of what should reasonably be allowed.

The appeal is usually decided by an inspector who has been appointed by the Secretary of State to determine the appeal. The appeal process involves a public local inquiry or written representations. There is a further right of appeal to the High Court limited to points of law.[46]

Where it has been decided as a result of an enforcement notice appeal that no breach of planning control had taken place, the local planning authority is estopped from issuing another enforcement notice in respect of the same matter. In *Thrasyvoulou v SSE*,[47] the Court of Appeal decided that issue estoppel applied in planning law so that the local planning authority could not issue enforcement notices alleging breach of planning control where it has previously been decided in enforcement notice proceedings that there had been no breach of planning control and there had been no subsequent change of use in the premises. In that case the same use was being enforced against in both proceedings and there had not been an intervening change of use. No circumstances had been raised to make it fair or just for the proceedings to be re-opened.

In certain situations, the local planning authority may prohibit the carrying out of activities on land before an enforcement notice takes effect. A stop notice may be served in addition to an enforcement notice where the local planning authority considers it expedient to prevent, before the expiry of the period allowed for compliance with the notice, the carrying out of any activity which is sought to be enforced against in the enforcement notice.[48] However, a stop notice cannot prohibit the use of any building as a dwelling-house, or the use of land as the site of a caravan occupied by any person as his only or main residence. Nor can a stop notice prohibit the taking of any steps specified in the enforcement notice as required to be taken to remedy the breach of planning control, or the carrying out of an activity on land where the period during which it has been carried out (whether continuously or otherwise) began more than twelve months previously unless that activity is, or is incidental to, building, engineering, mining or other operations or the deposit of refuse or waste materials.[49]

A stop notice may not take effect (and so cannot be contravened) until such date as it may specify, being a date not earlier than three or later than twenty-eight days from the date of service.[50] A stop notice ceases to have effect either when the enforcement notice is withdrawn or quashed, or when the period for compliance with the enforcement notice expires or when the stop notice itself is withdrawn.[51] Breaches of enforcement notices or stop notices which have taken effect involve criminal offences.[52]

The Government stresses that enforcement action should not be undertaken unless there are good reasons. An enforcement notice should only be issued if the local planning authority considers it expedient to do so. The fact that an activity is a non-conforming use is not a sufficient reason in itself for taking enforcement action.[53] The Government has advised local planning authorities:

It is clearly undesirable that development should be carried out in advance of any necessary planning permission being obtained. Nothing in this circular should be taken as condoning a wilful breach of planning law. However, the power to issue an enforcement notice alleging that there has been a breach of planning control is entirely discretionary and is only to be used if the authority 'consider it expedient to do so having regard to the provisions of the development plan and to any other material considerations'. This permissive power should be used, in regard to either operational development or material changes of use, only where planning reasons clearly warrant such action, and there is no alternative to enforcement proceedings. Where the activity involved is one which would not give rise to insuperable planning objections if it were carried out somewhere else, then the planning authority should do all it can to help in finding suitable alternative premises before initiating enforcement action.[54]

Further advice has been given about alternatives to enforcement action:

Local planning authorities have powers to take enforcement action when they are satisfied that there has been a breach of planning control. In dealing with small businesses, it is particularly important that authorities should explore alternatives to enforcement action. If it eventually proves impossible to reach a satisfactory compromise and enforcement action has to be taken, it should follow a carefully planned timetable which will give the operator of the enterprise time to obtain new premises. Every effort should be made to help the operator to obtain a suitable alternative site and local planning authorities should consider exercising their discretion to extend the period for compliance where this will avoid the disruption of production and permanent loss of employment.[55]

References

1. Town and Country Planning Act ('TCPA') 1971, s.22(1).
2. *Williams v MHLG* (1967) 18 P&CR 514.
3. *Lewis v SSE* (1971) 23 P&CR 125 at p. 128.
4. *Williams v MHLG* (1967) 18 P&CR 514 at p. 518.
5. TCPA 1971, s.22(2) (f).
6. Town and Country Planning (Use Classes) Order ('UCO') 1987 (No. 764).
7. Town and Country Planning General Development Order 1988 (No. 1813).
8. Local Government, Planning and Land Act 1980, Schedule 32; TCPA 1971, s.24A.

9. Government White Paper: Lifting the Burden, Cmnd. 9571, para. 3.6.
10. Ibid., para. 3.2.
11. Ibid., para. 3.6.
12. TCPA 1971, s.23(1).
13. TCPA 1971, s.22(1).
14. TCPA 1971, s.1.
15. TCPA 1971, s.29(1).
16. TCPA 1971, s.6.
17. Ibid., s.11.
18. Local Government Act ('LGA') 1985, Schedule 1.
19. The Future of Development Plans: Cm 569.
20. Circular 14/85, para. 5; see also PPG1, para. 14.
21. TCPA 1971, s.29(1).
22. Circular 22/80, para. 12.
23. Ibid., para. 13.
24. Circular 16/84, para. 13.
25. Circular 14/85, para. 3.
26. Circular 2/86, para. 12.
27. PPG 4, paras. 9 and 10.
28. Circular 16/87, para. 8: see also PPG 7, paras. 18 and 19.
29. Circular 8/87, para. 22.
30. Circular 8/87, paras. 19 and 20.
31. Circular 8/87, para. 23.
32. TCPA 1971, s.36.
33. Ibid., s.36(3).
34. Ibid., Schedule 9.
35. Ibid., s.35.
36. Circular 2/81, para. 15.
37. TCPA 1971, s.245.
38. TCPA 1971, s.87.
39. TCPA 1971, s. 88.
40. TCPA 1971, s.87(5).
41. *Howard v SSE* [1975] QB 235; *Lenlyn v SSE* [1984] JPL 482.
42. TCPA 1971, s.88(10).
43. *R v Kuxhaus* [1988] 2 WLR 1005; [1988] 2 PLR 59.
44. TCPA 1971, s.88.
45. TCPA 1971, s.87(4).
46. TCPA 1971, s.246.
47. [1988] 3 WLR 1; [1988] 2 PLR 37.
48. TCPA 1971, s.90.
49. TCPA 1971, s.90(2).
50. TCPA 1971, s.90(3).
51. TCPA 1971, s.90(4).
52. TCPA 1971, ss.89 and 90(7).
53. Circular 22/80, para. 13.
54. Circular 22/80, para. 15.
55. PPG 4, para. 19.

2 CONDITIONS AND AGREEMENTS

Planning conditions and agreements can severely restrict the use of land. Planning conditions are attached to the planning permission. If the permission is implemented, the conditions attached will regulate the use of the land. Similarly the owner of land and the local planning authority may enter into a planning agreement for the purpose of restricting or regulating the development or use of that land.[1] Such planning agreements are often entered into before planning permission is granted and can have a serious effect on the possible uses to which the land can be put.

This chapter outlines how conditions and agreements may restrict uses to which premises may be put. The particular problem of how far conditions may restrict the operation of the Use Classes Order is dealt with in detail in Chapter 5.

Conditions

The local planning authority can grant planning permission either unconditionally or subject to such conditions as it thinks fit.[2] However, these wide terms do not mean that the power to impose conditions is unfettered. There is a right of appeal to the Secretary of State against the imposition of such conditions on the planning permission.[3] Applications may now be made for planning permission to develop land without complying with conditions subject to which a previous planning permission was granted.[4] An application may also be made to retain buildings or works or continue the use of the land, without complying with some condition subject to which a previous planning permission was granted.[5]

Furthermore, the courts have repeatedly said that the discretion to impose conditions is not unlimited. In *Pyx Granite Co. Ltd v Minister of Housing and Local Government*, Lord Denning said:

> Although the planning authorities are given very wide powers to impose 'such conditions as they think fit', nevertheless the law says that those conditions, to be valid, must fairly and reasonably relate to the permitted development. The planning authority are not at liberty to use their powers for an ulterior object, however desirable that object may seem to them to be in the public interest. If they mistake or misuse their powers, however *bona fide*, the court can interfere by declaration and injunction. . . .[6]

Viscount Dilhorne in *Newbury District Council v Secretary of State for the Environment*[7] endorsed this statement and said:

> It followed that the conditions imposed must be for a planning purpose and not for any ulterior one and that they must fairly and reasonably relate to the development permitted. Also they must not be so unreasonable that no reasonable planning authority could have imposed them.

In addition to the high court strictures, government advice is that conditions should not be imposed unless they are both necessary and effective, and do not place unjustifiable burdens on applicants. Circular 1/85 goes on to say that conditions should only be imposed where they are:

(a) necessary,
(b) relevant to planning,
(c) relevant to the development permitted,
(d) enforceable,
(e) precise,
(f) reasonable in all other respects.[8]

Conditions Restricting Use

A planning condition may restrict a lawful use and restrict the applicant's rights under the Use Classes Order.[9] However, where a local planning authority intends to exclude the operation of the Use Classes Order, it should say so by the imposition of a condition in unequivocal terms.[10] It is possible to restrict changes of use which would not be regarded as development either because the change is not material or because of the Use Classes Order.[11] However there is a general presumption against limiting the application of the Use Classes Order in a particular case, and it would be contrary to the general principles of control for an authority to prevent such permitted development or other changes of use by the widespread imposition of conditions.[12] There may occasionally be circumstances where such a condition can be justified such as restricting changes of use so as to prevent the use of large retail premises as a food or convenience goods supermarket where such a use might generate an unacceptable level of additional traffic, or so as to limit the storage of hazardous substances in a warehouse.[13]

Conditions restricting ancillary or incidental activities are discouraged. Such conditions should not normally be imposed on permissions for manufacturing or service industry, except where they are designed to preclude or regulate activities giving rise to hazard, noise or offensive emissions.[14]

Personal Permissions

A permission may be made subject to a condition that it shall inure only for the benefit of a named person – usually the applicant. However, it is seldom desirable to impose such a condition and it will scarcely ever be justified in the case of a permission for the erection of a permanent building. There are exceptional occasions where permission may be granted for the use of a building or land for some purpose which would not normally be allowed at the site, simply because there are strong compassionate or other personal grounds for so doing.[15]

Personal permissions arise on their peculiar facts. A local planning authority has granted a personal permission for a farmer to use the kiosk of an adjoining filling station that had closed down for the sale of agricultural produce grown on his own land.[16] The Secretary of State has granted a personal and temporary permission to allow a lady in her seventies to live in a mobile home.[17] Where a personal condition has been imposed contrary to government advice, it is likely to be removed on appeal. For example, a personal condition imposed on a DIY retail development for the benefit of a named company was removed by the inspector as it could not be justified in the light of the advice contained in Circular 1/85.[18] In a further case involving a non-retail warehouse,[19] the inspector similarly refused to impose a personal condition as again it could not be justified in the light of government advice.

Occupancy Conditions on Commercial or Industrial Property

Conditions are sometimes imposed restricting the occupation of commercial or industrial premises to local firms. Circular 1/85 gives firm advice that such conditions should not be imposed except where the need for expansion of a local firm is sufficient to justify a departure from the general restraint policy applying in an area, and that in such a case it may be essential to ensure that a permission granted under such circumstances will not be abused. Otherwise such conditions are regarded as undesirable.[20]

The Secretary of State has struck out such conditions on appeal when they have been imposed by the local planning authority.[21] In a South Buckinghamshire case, he struck out the condition and stated that Circular 1/85 was regarded as a material consideration weightier than the previously approved structure plan policy.[22] Local planning authorities who continue to impose such conditions contrary to the advice in the circular are at risk for costs on appeal.[23]

In another case involving South Buckinghamshire,[24] the inspector struck out an occupancy condition even though he was of the opinion that the original application for commercial development should have been refused in the light of the general presumption against commercial development in that area. The inspector accepted that the additional office floor space would tend to increase the demand for development but, in his view, that demand was created when offices were permitted and could not be dissipated by a condition restricting their occupancy. In a further case in Redhill,[25] the local planning authority argued that the condition requiring the occupation of the proposed offices by local firms was necessary to prevent firms moving in from outside the area, thus increasing the demand for housing, and hence the pressure on the green belt. The inspector noted that the original permission had not been granted to meet the specific needs of local firms. He found that the condition was not necessary as he was not persuaded that the use of the proposed offices by a firm outside the area would necessarily result in more pressure on housing and on the green belt than would the occupancy of the proposed offices by a local firm given the good rail routes and good and improving road links in the area.

Local occupancy conditions have, however, still been imposed. In a case in Haywards Heath, an occupancy condition was imposed for 50,000 sq. ft. of offices even though the report of the case does not point to the need for expansion of a particular local firm.[26] In a case concerning a proposed four-storey office building and car park in Maidenhead,[27] the inspector imposed a local occupancy condition but the appellant was a firm already established in the area where it needed to remain to ensure continuity of building and staff. The inspector found that the need for the expansion of a local business was sufficient to justify a departure from the general restraint policy applicable to the area.

A permission was granted for the development of seven industrial units at Littlemore, Oxford, subject to a local occupancy condition which was upheld on appeal. An appeal was made to the High Court against the reasoning of the inspector who upheld the planning appeal.[28] However, the question as to whether the condition should have been imposed in the light of the advice given in Circular 1/85 was not allowed to be raised in the high court proceedings.

In a further case, a London borough sought to impose a condition restricting office occupation to particular kinds of occupier, such as accountants, architects, surveyors, solicitors, insurance office, insurance brokers, employment agency and estate agency.[29] The council wanted to provide for a range of uses which could not compete for alternative premises, particularly in purpose-built blocks, because of higher rent levels or letting management policies. The inspector recognised that the condition put a severe limitation on the owner to finance the proposed development and to dispose of the property. He found the condition to be unduly restrictive and against national policy as expressed in Circular 1/85.

Domestic Occupancy Conditions

Government policy states that conditions restricting the occupancy of houses to a particular type of person (e.g. to those already living or working in the area or holiday-makers) should not be imposed save in the more exceptional circumstances where there are clear and specific circumstances that warrant allowing an individual house (or extension) on a site where development would not normally be permitted.[30]

The Secretary of State allowed an appeal against an occupancy condition imposed on a new dwelling by the local planning authority who was concerned about 'a possible proliferation of second homes to the detriment of the Welsh way of life'. The Secretary of State endorsed the inspector's conclusion that the description of 'the most exceptional circumstances' could not be applied in that case, which was unlikely to be an isolated one.[31]

Agricultural Occupancy Conditions

Conditions may be imposed on planning permissions for dwellings to be built to house agricultural or forestry workers. Such conditions are not unreasonable.[32] To justify such a permission, the applicant will normally have to establish the need for a dwelling on the farm before planning permission will be given; even then care should be taken to choose a site which is well related to existing farm buildings.[33] Where such a condition has been appropriately imposed, it will not normally be removed on a subsequent application unless it is shown that the long-term needs for dwellings for agricultural workers, both on the farm and in the locality, no longer warrant its reservation for that purpose.[34] However the Government now acknowledges that changes in the scale and character of agriculture in response to market changes may well affect the requirement for dwellings by agricultural or forestry workers. Circular 16/87 goes on to state:

> Such dwellings should not be kept vacant simply by virtue of planning conditions restricting occupancy which have outlived their usefulness. Applications for the removal of such conditions should be considered on the basis of realistic assessments of the continuing need for them. There is no virtue in keeping dwellings unoccupied if they are no longer needed for their original purpose.[35]

This advice has been said to be a recognition that the circumstances needed to justify a removal of an agricultural occupancy condition are now more frequently likely to be met, rather than any indication that the required circumstances should themselves be relaxed.[36]

In practice, it will often be necessary for the applicant to show that there is no agricultural need for the dwelling in question. This can be done by placing the dwelling on the market at a price reflecting its condition.[37] The vacancy of other such dwellings will also point to lack of demand. Against such evidence will be weighed demand for such dwellings as evidenced by recent applications for nearby dwellings. However such applications may only show a need for farm workers to live on particular farms rather than in the locality itself.

Temporary Permissions

Planning permission may be granted subject to conditions, requiring, for instance, the removal of a building or works authorised by the permission, or the discontinuance of any use of land so authorised at the end of a specified period, or the carrying out of any works required for the reinstatement of land at the end of that period.[38] A temporary permission will normally only be appropriate either where the applicant himself proposes temporary development, or when a trial run is needed in order to assess the effect of the development on the area.[39] A temporary condition will not be justified to protect future development unless there are firm proposals to develop the site.[40] Occasionally it may be acceptable to limit the use of land for a particular purpose to certain seasons of the year. Such conditions may for example be appropriate for holiday caravans and chalets.[41]

In Westminster, certain office premises have been operating under a series of temporary permissions since the Second World War. These premises are in the Mayfair, Queen Anne Street and Gloucester Place areas of Westminster. The temporary permissions are due to expire up to and including 1990 and the Westminster local plan contains policies normally to require the reversion to residential use of formerly residential premises in temporary office use at the expiry of the temporary planning permission.[42] Despite questions being asked about the appropriateness of the policies in the light of government advice, appeals have been dismissed against the refusal to remove the temporary conditions.[43] The special character of Mayfair has been said to be an important consideration in justifying the policy.

Planning Agreements

In addition to the power to impose conditions, the local planning authority may enter into an agreement with any person interested in land in their area for the purpose of restricting or regulating the development or use of the land.[44] Such an agreement is often called a 'section 52 agreement'. The agreement may contain certain incidental and consequential provisions (including provisions of a financial character) that appear to the local planning authority to be necessary or expedient for the purposes of the agreement. A section 52 agreement may be enforced by the local planning authority against persons deriving title from the covenantor in respect of that land.[45]

It is not necessarily easy for a landowner to obtain a discharge of a section 52 agreement. In respect of modern agreements, there is no right to apply to the Secretary of State for a discharge of the terms of the agreement.[46] The landowner must treat with the local planning authority to obtain a modification or discharge of the agreement. If he fails he can seek the modification or discharge of the agreement by making an application to the Lands Tribunal under s.84 of the Law of Property Act 1925.[47] The grounds upon which an order can be made by the Lands Tribunal are limited.[48] The fact that the Secretary of State may have granted planning permission is not conclusive.[49] The Lands Tribunal can only make an order discharging or modifying the covenant where it is satisfied that one of four grounds applies:

1. that the restriction ought to be deemed obsolete by reason of changes in the character of the property or the neighbourhood or other circumstances of the case;
2. that some reasonable use of the land would be impeded where the restriction did not serve any practical benefits of substantial value or advantage to persons entitled to the benefit of the covenant or where the restriction was contrary to the public interest: under this ground money should be adequate compensation for any loss or disadvantage (if any) suffered by the persons enjoying the benefit of the covenant;
3. that those entitled to the benefit of the restriction have agreed to the discharge or modification; or
4. that the proposed discharge or modification would not injure the persons entitled to the benefit of the restriction.[50]

The Lands Tribunal will discharge or modify a restrictive covenant deemed obsolete. In one case it modified a covenant that an extension would be occupied by domestic staff employed for service in the house by substituting a covenant to prohibit the use of the extension except for a person or persons employed solely or mainly in agriculture.[51]

The question arises whether the local planning authority should seek to restrict the use by entering a section 52 agreement or by imposing a condition where both may be considered appropriate. Circular 1/85 advises that in such cases the local planning authority should impose a condition rather than seek to deal with the matter by means of the making of an agreement, since the imposition of restrictions by means of an agreement deprives the developer of the opportunity of seeking to have the restrictions varied or removed by an application or appeal if they subsequently become inappropriate or too onerous.[52]

References

1. TCPA 1971, s.52.
2. TCPA 1971, s.29(1).
3. Ibid., s.36.
4. Ibid., s.31A.
5. Ibid., s.32.
6. [1958] 1 QB 554, at p. 572.
7. [1980] JPL 325, at p. 327.
8. Circular 1/85, para. 11, PPG1, para. 24.
9. *City of London Corporation v S.O.S.E.* (1971) 23 P&CR 169.
10. *Carpet Decor (Guildford) Ltd v S.O.S.E. and Guildford BC* [1981] JPL 806.
11. Circular 1/85, para. 66.
12. Ibid., para. 67.
13. Ibid., para. 68.
14. Circular 1/85, para. 71.
15. Circular 1/85, para. 73.
16. [1984] JPL 835.
17. [1974] JPL 496.
18. *Enfield LBC* and *B and Q (Retail) Ltd* (1986) 1 PAD 453.
19. *Worcester CC* and *Frincon Holdings* (1987) 2 PAD 76.
20. Circular 1/85, paras. 74–5.
21. [1985] JPL 898.
22. Ibid., at p. 901.
23. Circular 2/87, para. 13.
24. *South Bucks DC* and *Holland Automation International* (1985) 1 PAD 159.
25. [1986] JPL 702; see also [1988] JPL 587.
26. [1986] JPL 698.
27. *Windsor and Maidenhead RBC* and *Lambart Computing* (1986) 1 PAD 162.
28. *Slough Industrial Estates v SSE* [1987] JPL 353.
29. [1986] JPL 703.
30. Circular 1/85, para. 77.
31. [1986] JPL 388; see also [1986] JPL 390.
32. *Fawcett Properties v Buckingham CC* [1961] AC 674.
33. Circular 24/73 Annex, para. 4.
34. Circular 24/73 Annex, para. 14: Circular 16/85, para. 8.
35. Circular 16/87, para. 9.
36. [1988] JPL 848, 849.
37. K. Smith, 'The agricultural condition of occupancy revisited', JPL, 1986, p. 416.
38. TCPA 1971, s.39 (1).
39. Circular 1/85, para. 83.
40. [1984] JPL 905.
41. Circular 1/85, para. 87.
42. City of Westminster District Plan (1982) para. 10.59.
43. *Westminster City Council* and *Radio Luxembourg* (1986) 1 PAD 429; the Brook House case APP/x 5990/A/85/038324; see also *Niarchos v SSE* (1978) 35 P&CR 259; *Niarchos v SSE* (No 2) [1981] JPL 118.
44. TCPA 1971, s.52.

45. Ibid., s.52(2).
46. An application may be made to the Secretary of State to remove a restriction imposed in agreements made under TCPA 1932, s.34, on the ground that the restriction is inconsistent with the proper planning or development of the area. There is also a right to refer the agreement to arbitration: TCPA 1971 Schedule 24, para. 87.
47. As amended by the Law of Property Act ('LPA') 1969, s.28. See *Re Beecham Group Ltd's Application* (1980) 41 P&CR 369.
48. See *Abbey Homesteads (Development) Ltd v Northamptonshire CC* (1986) 278 EG 1249.
49. *Re Martin's Application* [1987] JPL 43, affirmed C.A. [1988] 3 PLR 45; *Re Kentwood's Application* [1987] JPL 137.
50. LPA 1925, s.84 as amended by LPA 1969, s.28.
51. *Re Cox's Application* [1985] JPL 564.
52. Circular 1/85, para. 10.

3 MATERIAL CHANGE OF USE

Planning permission is required on the making of any material change in the use of any buildings or other land, as such a change of use constitutes development.[1] The change of use must either in the kind of use or in the degree of use be material from a planning point of view[2] for a material change of use to occur.[3] Whether a change of use has occurred in a particular case is a matter of fact and degree.

What has to be considered is the character of the use of the land, that is to say, the character of the activities carried on upon it. The following are therefore irrelevant in determining what the use was or may become:[4]

    (a) the identity of the occupier or person who carries on the activities;[5]
    (b) the particular purpose why he carries on those activities;[6]
    (c) the ownership or source of supply of any materials employed in those activities;
    (d) the destination elsewhere of the products of those activities; and
    (e) activities elsewhere even if related to activities on the land in question.[7]

A change in the type of goods sold on land will also not normally amount to a material change of use.[8] However, although all those matters are irrelevant in themselves, it may well be that some at least are capable of illustrating the character of activities undertaken on the land.[9]

Changes of use falling within the Use Classes Order do not amount to development, and no planning permission is necessary for such changes. Chapter 5 and succeeding chapters deal with the Use Classes Order.

Primary and Ancillary Uses

There is no material change of use if ancillary uses are introduced on land provided that the primary use of the land does not change. However, the ancillary use is only protected so long as there is no material change or abandonment of the primary use. Therefore a hotel use may embrace a number of ancillary uses such as a bar used extensively by non-residents.[10] A caravan may be parked in the curtilage of a dwelling-house provided it is used as an adjunct to the use of that dwelling-house.[11] A private car may be repaired in a domestic garage but a commercial activity of repairing cars cannot take place there.[12] Farm products produced on the farm may be sold on that farm but not products from elsewhere.[13]

However, if the ancillary use changes to being a primary use in its own right there will be a material change of use. The viewing of films in a shop was held to be a use separate from a shop.[14] Similarly the parking of a caravan capable of being used as an independent residential unit has been held to be a material change of use.[15] The use of premises as a night club was regarded as a separate use from that of a restaurant.[16]

Intensification

A use may be intensified to such an extent that there has been a material change of use from the previous use. In *Brooks & Burton Ltd v S.O.S.E.*,[17] Lawton LJ affirmed the general view that intensification of use could amount to a material change of use: whether it was or not depended upon the degree of intensification. However intensification within a Use Class would not amount to a material change of use provided that the use remains within that class.[18]

Material changes of use have occurred when land previously used for the parking of one or two lorries was used for the parking of thirty-five to forty lorries;[19] when land formerly used to store two caravans was used to store forty[20] and where land used for a little open stacking was used for twenty stacks, some reaching heights of between twenty-five and thirty feet.[21]

Dual and Composite Uses

A composite or dual use occurs where separate uses are being carried out on a planning unit. It has been suggested that a dual use occurs where there is a geographical separation of uses and a composite use occurs where there is no such separation[22] but it is doubtful whether this distinction can be rigidly applied. Where one of the two uses ceases that will not amount to a material change of use unless there has been an intensification of the other use.[23]

The situation of two or more primary uses on a site must be distinguished from that where there is a primary and ancillary user. In the latter case, the cessation of a primary use is likely to bring about a material change of use of the land from a former primary use to a new primary use.[24] A site may however have recurrent uses where the uses are interchanged. There may be seasonal or intermittent changes such as to grazing in winter and camping in summer.[25]

The Planning Unit

One has to look at the whole planning unit in assessing whether a material change in the use of a building or other land has occurred. (As a building is defined to include part of a building,[26] the planning unit may consist of part of a building.) If a restaurant were placed in a department store to serve the customers of that store, it would be considered part and parcel of the planning unit of the department store and its use as ancillary to the store. However, a physically distinct restaurant on the ground floor with separate entrances would be considered a separate planning unit with a separate use.

Three tests were propounded by Bridge J in *Burdle v S.O.S.E.*[27] in assessing what the planning unit would be in a given situation:

> First, that whenever it is possible to recognise a single main purpose of the occupier's use of his land to which secondary activities are incidental or ancillary, the whole unit of occupation should be considered. . . . But, secondly, it may equally be apt to consider the entire unit of occupation even though the occupier carries on a variety of activities and it is not possible to say that one is incidental or ancillary to another. This is well settled in the case of a composite use where the component activities fluctuate in their intensity from time to time but the different activities are not confined within separate and physically distinct areas of land.
>
> Thirdly, however, it may frequently occur that within a single unit of occupation two or more physically separate and distinct areas are occupied for substantially different and unrelated purposes. In such a case each area used for a different main purpose (together with its incidental and ancillary activities) ought to be considered as a separate planning unit.

The Timing of the Change

Questions arise as to when change of use can be said to have occurred. The courts have said that the question is one of fact and degree in each case. A change of use may occur when the building is being fitted out for its new uses.[28] On the other hand, the courts have insisted that the new use should be genuine and should take place for more than a minimal period. In *Kwik Save Discount Group v S.O.S.W.*,[29] a token use of the site for one month was held not to involve a material change of use taking place.

Dwelling-houses

No development is deemed to have taken place involving the use of any buildings or other land within the curtilage of a dwelling-house for any purpose incidental to the enjoyment of the dwelling-house as such.[30] However, it has also been declared for the avoidance of doubt that the use as two or more separate dwelling-houses of any building previously used as a single dwelling-house involves a material change in the use of the building and each part thereof which is so used.[31]

In ascertaining what is the curtilage of the dwelling-house the land must serve the purpose of the house or building in some necessary or reasonable way.[32] However there will be a material change of use on agricultural land if it is added to the curtilage of the dwelling-house.[33] The building or land can only be used if it is incidental to the enjoyment of the dwelling-house. It is not incidental to the enjoyment of a dwelling-house if a separate use is taking place. In one case, a car enthusiast was repairing his family's and other cars within the curtilage of his dwelling-house. The inspector found that repairing his family's cars was incidental to the enjoyment of the dwelling-house but the repairing of other cars was not.[34] Similarly the parking of a commercial lorry in the curtilage of a dwelling-house has been held to be not incidental to its use.[35]

The use of two or more separate dwelling-houses involves a material change of use if the previous use was as a single dwelling-house.[36] Planning permission is therefore necessary to divide a dwelling-house into separate flats or maisonettes. This provision also catches the further division of an already divided dwelling-house.[37] Multiple occupation alone does not involve separate dwelling-houses[38] but there may be an intensification of use by such multiple occupation.[39]

Greater London

A provision which only relates to Greater London deems the use as temporary sleeping accommodation of any residential premises in Greater London to involve a material change of use of the premises and each part thereof which is so used.[40] 'Use as temporary sleeping accommodation' in this context means use as sleeping accommodation which is occupied by the same person for less than ninety consecutive nights and which is provided for a consideration arising either by way of trade for money or money's worth or by reason of the employment of the occupant (whether or not the relationship of landlord and tenant is thereby created). 'Residential premises' means a building, or any part of a building, which was previously used, or was designed or constructed for use, as one or more permanent residences.

The purpose of this provision is to preserve existing housing stock and prevent its being used to accommodate transient visitors. A condition imposed on hostel accommodation that the majority of lettings should be for a period of not less than twenty-two days was upheld where the twenty-two-day period was inserted to ensure that hostels would not be used as temporary sleeping accommodation.[41] (The twenty-two-day period has now been extended to ninety days in the legislation concerning temporary sleeping accommodation.) The use of premises as temporary sleeping accommodation has been described as tantamount to use as a hostel.[42] But temporary sleeping accommodation covers other uses such as using property for short-term let accommodation.[43]

A further provision which relates only to Greater London provides that there is a material change of use of a dwelling-house if it becomes subject to a time-sharing scheme.[44] In this context, a dwelling-house (which may include a flat) becomes subject to a time-sharing scheme when any person is granted a right entitling him to occupy the dwelling-house or any part of it for a specified week or other period in every year during which the right subsists.

Tipping

The deposit of refuse or waste materials on land involves a material change of use, notwithstanding that the land is comprised in a site already used for that purpose, if either the superficial area of the deposit is thereby extended, or the height of the deposit is thereby extended and exceeds the level of land adjoining the site.[45]

Advertisements

The use for the display of advertisements of any external part of a building which is not normally used for that purpose is treated as involving a material change of use.[46] However planning permission is deemed to be granted where the display of advertisements is in accordance with the advertisement regulations.[47]

References

1. TCPA 1971, s.22(1), 23(1).
2. *East Barnet UDC v BTC* [1962] 2 QB 484 at p. 490; *Devonshire CC v Allens (Caravans) Estates Ltd* (1962) 14 P&CR 440 at p. 441.
3. Circular 67/49, para. 4 (iii) (no longer in force).
4. *London Residuary Body v SSE* [1988] 2 PLR 79 at p. 85 (per Simon Brown J).
5. *Lewis v SSE* (1971) 23 P&CR 144 at p. 147.
6. *Snook v SSE* (1977) 33 P&CR 1.
7. *Westminster CC v British Waterways Board* (1985) 49 P&CR 117 at p. 125.
8. *Marshall v Nottingham Corporation* [1960] 1 WLR 707 at p. 717.
9. *London Residuary Body v SSE* [1988] 2 PLR 79 at p. 85 (per Simon Brown J).
10. *Emma Hotels Ltd v S.O.S.E.* [1979] JPL 390; [1981] JPL 283.
11. [1976] JPL 586.
12. [1976] JPL 530; *Peake v S.O.S.W.* (1971) 22 P&CR 859.
13. *Williams v MHLG* (1967) 18 P&CR 514.
14. *Lydcare Ltd v S.O.S.E.* [1984] JPL 809.

15. [1978] JPL 489.
16. *Trio Thames Ltd v S.O.S.E.* [1984] JPL 183.
17. [1977] JPL 720, 723.
18. Ibid.
19. [1967] JPL 292.
20. [1969] JPL 705.
21. [1974] JPL 100.
22. M. Grant, *Urban Planning Law*, Sweet & Maxwell, 1986, p. 171.
23. *Wipperman v Barking LBC* (1965) 17 P&CR 225; *Philglow Ltd v S.O.S.E.* [1985] JPL 318.
24. *David W. Barking Ltd v S.O.S.E.* [1980] JPL 594.
25. *Webber v M.H.L.G.* [1968] 1 WLR 29.
26. TCPA 1971, s.290.
27. [1972] 3 AER 240, 244.
28. *Backer v S.O.S.E.* (1984) 47 P&CR 149.
29. [1981] JPL 198.
30. TCPA 1971, s.22(2) (d).
31. Ibid., s.22(3) (a).
32. *Sinclair-Lockhart's Trustees v Central Land Board* (1950) 1 P&CR 195, affirmed (1951) 1 P&CR 320.
33. *Sampson's Executors v Nottinghamshire CC* [1949] 2 KB 439.
34. [1980] JPL 472. But see [1988] JPL 837, where the keeping of over forty dogs as a hobby resulted in a material change of use for the dwelling-house.
35. [1978] JPL 789; [1988] JPL 202.
36. TCPA 1971, s.22(3)(a).
37. See definition of 'building' to include part of a building: TCPA 1971, s.290.
38. *Ealing Corporation v Ryan* [1965] 2 QB 486.
39. *R v M.H.L.G. exp. Habib Ullah* [1964] 1 QB 178.
40. Greater London Council (General Powers) Act 1973, s.25 as amended by the Greater London Council (General Powers) Act 1983, s.4.
41. *Commercial and Residential Property Development Co v SSE* [1982] JPL 513.
42. [1986] JPL 451.
43. *Westminster City Council* and *Peter* (1988) 3 PAD 109. See also Park West decision: T/APP/C/87/X5990/P6.
44. Greater London Council (General Powers) Act 1984, s.5.
45. TCPA 1971, s.22(3)(b).
46. TCPA 1971, s.22(4).
47. TCPA 1971, s.64; Town and Country Planning (Control of Advertisements) Regulations 1984 (SI No. 421).

4 LAWFUL AND ESTABLISHED USES

It is important to be able to ascertain what uses may lawfully be carried on and what uses cannot be enforced against. Planning law draws a distinction between lawful uses and established uses. Lawful uses are those which have been recognised or permitted under the planning legislation. Established uses are those which cannot be enforced against but need not be permitted. In addition to lawful and established uses, this chapter also looks at the question of when use rights may have been abandoned.

Lawful Uses

A planning use is unlawful if it began in contravention of planning control after 1 July 1948.[1] In order that the use of the land should be lawful, it should have either been subsisting on 1 July 1948 and have continued since[2] or planning permission should have been granted for it.[3] A use of the land will not be unlawful merely owing to failure to comply with a condition attached to the permission unless that condition was a condition precedent.[4]

Established Uses

A use of land is established and therefore free from enforcement action if:

1. it was begun before the beginning of 1964 without planning permission and has continued since the end of 1963; or
2. it was begun before the beginning of 1964 under a planning permission in that behalf subject to conditions or limitations, which either have never been complied with or have not been complied with since the end of 1963; or
3. it was begun after the end of 1963 as a result of a change of use not requiring planning permission and there has been, since the end of 1963, no change of use requiring planning permission.[5]

Enforcement action can only be taken if it appears to the local planning authority that there has been a breach of planning control since the end of 1963.[6] However, an enforcement notice relating to certain breaches of planning control may only be issued within the period of four years from the date of the breach. These breaches mostly concern operational development but also include breaches involving use as a single dwelling-house. The breaches concerning dwelling-houses are the making without planning permission of a change of use of any building to use as a single dwelling-house or the failure to comply with a condition which prohibits or has the effect of preventing a change of use of a building to use as a single dwelling-house.[7]

Established Use Certificates

An application may be made to the local planning authority for an established use certificate by a person having an interest in the land.[8] The use of the land will be regarded as established if one of the three conditions regarding use subsisting since the end of 1964 is proved.[9] No application may be made in respect of the use of the land as a single dwelling-house or any use not subsisting at the time of the application.[10] Provided the use has not been abandoned, it may be taken to subsist even though it was not active at that time and may be held to have continued even though there has been no active use.[11] An established use certificate may be granted either for the whole land specified in the application or part of it and, in the case of an application specifying two or more uses, either for all those uses or for one or more of them.[12]

An established use certificate is conclusive of the matters which are stated in the document in respect of subsequent appeal proceedings if an enforcement notice is later issued in respect of activity on the site. On a subsequent appeal, the Secretary of State will look to the description of the activity in the established use certificate. If the description covers the activity being enforced against and there has been continuous use since, the Secretary of State will not be able to find that there has been a material change of use even if the activity has intensified since the date of the certificate. It is therefore important that the certificate defines the use and intensity with precision. In *Broxbourne Borough Council v S.O.S.E.*,[13] the court upheld the Secretary of State in not looking behind the certificate (which did not declare a limit on the use) to determine what intensity of use existed at the time that the certificate was issued. The purpose of the established use certificate was said to preclude the necessity of investigating events which might have occurred many years before as to what was the established use at the date of the certificate. The case demonstrates that planning authorities should exercise great care concerning the terms of established use certificates which they issue. If a certificate is not drawn with care and expressly limited to the precise use in question, the authority may find itself thereafter precluded from preventing a use for which planning permission would not have been granted simply because the certificate had been issued in terms wider than were necessary.

There is a right of appeal to the Secretary of State against the refusal or part refusal of an established use certificate.[14] Similarly, he may give directions requiring applications for established use certificates to be referred to him instead of being dealt with by local planning authorities.[15]

Reversion to Previous Uses

There are a number of situations where the land may lawfully revert to a previous use without the need for further planning permission. However, the previous use must be a lawful use. It will not be enough if the use is only established. *L.T.S.S. Print and Supply Services Ltd v Hackney LBC*[16] decided that the reversion must be a previous lawful use and that an established use was not necessarily a lawful use. Mere immunity from process did not make the act in itself lawful. Section 23 of the Town and Country Planning Act 1971 deals with situations when there may be a reversion to a lawful use. These are:

1. Where on 1 July 1948 land was being temporarily used for a purpose other than the purpose for which it was normally used, planning permission is not required for the resumption of the use of the land for the normal purpose before 6 December 1968. However the use resumed must be the 'normal' use. Such a use was lost after a 'temporary' use lasting twenty years.[17]

2. Where on 1 July 1948 land was normally used for one purpose and was also used on occasions, whether at regular intervals or not for any other purpose, planning permission is not required in respect of the use of the land on similar occasions before 6 December 1968 or in respect of the use of the land for that other purpose on similar occasions on or after that date if the land has been used for that other purpose on at least one similar occasion since 1 July 1948 and the beginning of 1968.[18]

3. Where land was unoccupied on 1 July 1948, but had before that day been occupied at some time on or after 7 January 1937, planning permission is not required in respect of any use of that land begun before 6 December 1968 for the purpose for which the land was last used before 1 July 1948.[19]

In the situations above the use of land as a caravan site shall not be treated as a use for which planning permission is not required, unless the land was so used on one occasion at least during the period of two years ending 9 March 1960.

4. Where planning permission to develop land has been granted for a limited period, planning permission is not required for the resumption at the end of that period of the use of the land for the purpose for which it was normally used before permission was granted.[20] The

former normal use must have been a lawful use.[21] This provision can be relied upon even though the use does not immediately cease at the end of the temporary period and even if there have been a succession of temporary permissions.[22]

5. Where by a development order planning permission to develop land has been granted subject to limitations, planning permission is not required for the use of that land which is the normal use of that land,[23] but the normal use must be a lawful use. A development order is an order made by the Secretary of State granting planning permission.[24] One of the orders, the General Development Order, is of wide ranging application and grants general planning permission subject to a number of conditions and limitations. In *Cynon Valley B.C. v S.O.S.W.*,[25] a fish and chip shop was used temporarily for the purposes of an antique shop. The change of use was permitted under the General Development Order which allowed a change of use from a fish and chip shop to a class limited to certain other shops. Owing to those limitations, the Court of Appeal held that the owner of the shop was entitled to rely on this provision to revert back to the previous lawful use. The class of shops and the deemed permission have now changed by reason of the new Use Classes and General Development Orders and it may be questioned whether the same result would still occur.

6. Where an enforcement notice has been issued in respect of development of land, planning permission is not required for the use of that land for the purpose for which it could lawfully have been used if that development had not been carried out.[26] To rely on this provision the previous use must have been a lawful use. A mere established use will not suffice.[27] Furthermore, the lawful use must have immediately preceded the use enforced against. In *Young v S.O.S.E.*,[28] the House of Lords held that the applicant was not allowed under this provision to follow the planning history of the land further back through its earlier uses until he got back to the last lawful use. If the last use was unlawful, there was then no purpose for which such land could be used without obtaining planning permission. Under this provision, there can be reversion to the last lawful use even if that use has been abandoned.[29]

It should be noted that there is no express provision allowing the reversion to a previous lawful use when a personal planning permission is no longer being relied upon. As has been seen, a condition may sometimes be imposed limiting the particular use to a named person. The question arises whether planning permission is needed to use the building when the person named no longer wishes to occupy it. In some cases, the terms of the planning permission may allow the reversion to a previous use. For example, a use can be considered within the terms of the planning permission where a condition has been imposed that the building may be used by a named individual for specified purposes, but when that use ceases, it should revert to the previous use. However, in other cases, it is likely that a new planning permission will be necessary to remove the offending condition and, if applicable, to permit a material change of use even if the proposed use is to be the same as the lawful use which subsisted before the use covered by the personal permission came into being.

Abandonment

The use of land instituted without the benefit of planning permission may be abandoned. There is now a number of cases in which this proposition has been upheld. In *Young v S.O.S.E.*[30] Watkins LJ said in the Court of Appeal:

> There was ample and powerful authority for the proposition which appeared . . . [in] the Encyclopedia of Planning Law and Practice that, when land ceases to be used for a lawful purpose for a period of time, it was a question of fact whether the right to use the land for that purpose has been abandoned so that the resumption of that use amounted to development requiring planning permission. Among other considerations in deciding whether abandonment has occurred was intention. . . .

Ceasing to use land for a particular purpose does not constitute a material change in the use of the land. However a use may become abandoned if it has ceased with no intention that it should be resumed.[31]

A period of non-use in itself will not normally give rise to abandonment. Land may be kept vacant with the intention that the use should one day be revived. A cessation of occupation for thirteen years has been held by the courts as not amounting to abandonment where the occupant had entered hospital.[32] Properties have been kept vacant for periods of up to thirty-five years without a finding that their use has been abandoned.[33] But the use of the property may be found to be abandoned if there is evidence that it was intended to abandon the use. In looking for such evidence the period of discontinuance, whether it was used for any other purpose and the owner's intentions in respect of the property will be relevant.[34] A cottage was held to be abandoned where it had been vacant for fifteen years, had been made uninhabitable to prevent squatting and had been used for agricultural purposes.[35] The use in another case was held to be abandoned[36] where a building had been vacant for twenty-six years and a substantial amount of demolition had taken place following a demolition order.

However, the doctrine of abandonment does not apply to a use pursuant to a planning permission. A grant of planning permission inures for the benefit of the land and of all persons for the time being interested in the land.[37] In *Pioneer Aggregates (UK) Ltd v S.O.S.E.*,[38] the House of Lords held that there was no principle of planning law that a valid planning permission capable of being implemented could be abandoned.

Use rights permitted under a planning permission may on the other hand be lost if a mutually inconsistent planning permission has been implemented. Where development was carried out which rendered one or other of the planning permissions incapable of implementation, the benefit of that permission was also lost.[39] Similarly, where the implementation of the permission has the effect of making a new planning unit, a lawful use under a previous planning permission may be lost. The existing use right disappeared because the character of the planning unit had been altered by the physical fact of the new development.[40] Furthermore, where a change of use has taken place, there will be no automatic right to revert to a previous use permitted by a planning permission unless the case falls within one of the specified cases where a reversion to a previous lawful use is allowed (see pp. 29–31, above).[41]

Discontinuance

The local planning authority may make a discontinuance order requiring the use of land to be discontinued or that conditions should be imposed on the continuance of a use of land.[42] An order under this provision shall not take effect unless it is confirmed by the Secretary of State, either without modification or subject to such modifications as he considers expedient.[43]

References

1. TCPA 1971, s.23 (10).
2. TCPA 1971, Schedule 24, para. 12.
3. TCPA 1971, s.23(1).
4. *Clwyd CC v S.O.S.W. and Welsh Aggregates* [1982] JPL 696; affirmed s.n. *Welsh Aggregates v S.O.S.E.* [1983] JPL 50.
5. TCPA 1971, s.94(1).
6. TCPA 1971, s.87(1).
7. TCPA 1971, s.87(4).
8. TCPA 1971, s.94(2).
9. TCPA 1971, s.94(1).
10. TCPA 1971, s.94(3).
11. [1981] JPL 449; [1982] JPL 800.
12. TCPA 1971, s.94(3).
13. [1980] QB 1.
14. TCPA 1971, s.95(2).

15. TCPA 1971, s.95(1).
16. [1976] 1 QB 663.
17. *Kingdom v MHLG* [1968] 1 QB 257.
18. TCPA 1971, s.23(3).
19. TCPA 1971, s.23(4).
20. TCPA 1971, s.23(5).
21. TCPA 1971, s.23(6); *Smith v S.O.S.E.* [1983] JPL 462.
22. *Smith v S.O.S.E.* [1983] JPL 462.
23. TCPA 1971, s.23(8).
24. TCPA 1971, s.24.
25. [1986] JPL 760.
26. TCPA 1971, s.23(9).
27. *L.T.S.S. Print and Supply Services v Hackney LBC* [1976] 1 QB 663.
28. *Young v S.O.S.E.* [1983] JPL 677.
29. *Fairchild v SSE* [1988] JPL 472.
30. [1983] JPL 465; affirmed [1983] JPL 677.
31. *Hartley v MHLG* [1970] 1 QB 413; see also *White v SSE, The Times*, 10 February 1989.
32. *Hale (dec'd) v Lichfield DC* noted [1979] JPL 425.
33. [1978] JPL 651; [1978] JPL 653; [1982] JPL 194; [1986] JPL 846.
34. [1986] JPL 846.
35. [1977] JPL 326.
36. [1987] JPL 849.
37. TCPA 1971, s.33(1).
38. [1985] AC 132.
39. *Pilkington v S.O.S.E.* [1973] 1 WLR 1527.
40. *Petticoat Lane Rentals v S.O.S.E.* [1971] 1 WLR 1112.
41. *Cynon Valley BC v S.O.S.W.* [1986] JPL 760; [1986] 2 EGLR 191; see also [1989] JPL 133.
42. TCPA 1971, s.51(1).
43. TCPA 1971, s.51(4).

5 THE USE CLASSES ORDER

The Use Classes Order was first introduced in 1948 to enable a variety of changes of use to occur without the need for planning permission. From 1948 to 1987 the Order stayed substantially in its original form although it was subject to some minor revisions. The Order was re-issued in 1972 and was subject to a minor amendment in 1983.[1] Following a study by the Property Advisory Group the Order was thoroughly revised in 1987 to fulfil its role as a deregulatory measure in line with the Government's aim to simplify the planning system and improve its efficiency.[2] The new Order contains fundamental and radical changes including the introduction of a new Business Class and a new Financial and Professional Services Class.[3]

Circular 13/87, Changes of Use of Buildings and Other Land, was issued at the same time as the new Order to explain it. It set out the two-fold aim of the Order:

(i) to reduce the number of classes while retaining effective control over changes of use which, because of environmental consequences or relationship with other uses, need to be subject to specific planning applications; and

(ii) to ensure that the scope of each class is wide enough to take in changes of use which generally do not need to be subject to specific control.[4]

It is also provided that a use which is included in and ordinarily incidental to any Use Class is not excluded from the use to which it is incidental merely because it is specified as a separate Use Class.[5] This provision protects ancillary uses. For example, an office within and ancillary to a department store would still fall within the Shops Class even though a pure office use would normally be considered to fall within the Business Class. In this respect it must be remembered that the Use Classes Order deals with the primary purpose of the land. Circular 13/87 advises that it is the main purpose which needs to be considered rather than simply looking to the amount of floor space occupied by different uses.[6]

Effect of the Order

Development is not involved, and therefore planning permission is not necessary, if buildings or other land used for a purpose specified in a class within the Use Classes Order are then used for any other purpose within the same Use Class.[7] Similarly, subject to the provisions of the Use Classes Order, any part of the land may be used for any other purpose within the same Use Class.[8] This provision enables the use of land to be switched from one use within a Use Class to another use within the same Use Class.

Land occupied with the building and used for the same purposes also enjoys the benefits of the Use Classes Order.[9] In this respect the new Order re-affirms the decision of *Brooks and Burton v S.O.S.E.*[10] which adopted a wide interpretation of a similar previous provision '. . . the test was what was the use to which the land occupied with the building had been put. If it had been used for the same purpose as the building it could be regarded planning-wise as one unit with the building; but if it had not been so used it could not be.'

Except for ancillary uses supporting the main use, the premises must be used for purposes within the Use Class and not for other purposes. In *Lydcare v S.O.S.E.*,[11] an attempt was made to combine a use falling within the Shops Class with a use involving the use by customers of viewing films in coin-operated booths. The Court of Appeal held that the viewing of films was a separate use which did not fall within the Use Class and upheld the enforcement notice in respect of that use. Similarly, in *Hussain v SSE*[12] an attempt was made to combine the keeping of chickens on site (for slaughtering in accordance with Muslim custom) with a shop. It was held that the keeping and slaughtering of chickens for commercial purposes could not be regarded as incidental to the use of the shop for retail trading, but as a separate use ancillary to or in the nature of use as a slaughterhouse. Lord Widgery LCJ said:

> In deciding whether it is ordinarily incidental to retail trade generally one has not to consider the special requirements of particular localities, particular areas and particular customers; the question has to be judged by looking at the shop as an activity as a whole and asking whether this new activity is one which is ordinarily incidental to the operation of keeping a retail shop. In my judgment the conclusion that it is not ordinarily incidental to the keeping and running of a retail shop is one which possibly cannot be avoided.

The Use Classes Order does not define all kinds of development. Sir Douglas Frank QC has pointed out that it is not uncommon to find that the definitions in the Order have been used as a shorthand to describe what is not being permitted. However, its intended purpose is to put outside the ambit of the Act a change of use which has taken place within the same Use Class.[13] Therefore, even if a change of use occurs which is not permitted by the Use Classes Order, it is still necessary to ask whether the change is material from a general planning point of view.

Even a change of use between two different Use Classes is not necessarily material. Where the change is not material, no development will be involved and therefore planning permission will not be necessary.

Conditions

It has already been seen that conditions attached to planning permissions may restrict the scope of rights under the Use Classes Order.[14] Similarly, such rights may be fettered if a section 52 planning agreement attaches to the property (see pp. 17–18, above).[15] Before relying on the terms of the Order, it is important to check that there is no condition attaching to planning permission or term in a section 52 agreement preventing reliance on the terms of the Order. For example, many light industrial premises have been given permission subject to a condition that they should be used for light industry only and for no other purpose. In such cases it will not be possible to rely on the provisions of the Order without having the condition removed beforehand.

However, there may be a reasonable prospect of having the condition removed by applying for planning permission to remove the effect of the condition.[16] Circular 13/87 advises local planning authorities to take account of the spirit of the new Order in considering applications for the removal of conditions limiting changes of use within one of the expanded classes. There is a presumption against conditions designed to negate the effects of the Order. The Secretary of State regards the imposition of such conditions as unreasonable unless there is clear evidence that the uses excluded would have serious adverse effects on the environment or on amenity, not susceptible to other control. Specific alternative conditions should be considered instead.[17] Unless there are environmental or amenity considerations involved, there is a reasonable likelihood of having the condition removed in an appeal against any decision by the local planning authority to impose such a condition or fail to remove it.

There have now been a number of cases in which conditions have been removed which sought to restrict the operation of the Use Classes Order. Some local planning authorities have sought to restrict premises to particular uses within Class B1 which groups certain office uses together with light industrial and research and development uses. Attempts have been made to restrict the use of premises to light industry in order to support local councils' policies. Alternatively conditions have been imposed restricting the areas of a building which can be used for office purposes. It has become clear that such conditions are unlikely to be upheld on appeal unless they can be justified to avoid serious effects on the environment or amenity.

Conditions attempting to nullify the effects of the Use Classes Order are unacceptable.[18] One such condition – which restricted the areas in the building which could be used for office, light industrial and research and development – was described as contrary to the spirit and letter of Circular 13/87 and no longer necessary or reasonable in that it restricted the freedom and flexibility given by the Use Classes and General Development Orders.[19] In another case, despite the local authority's case on the need to promote industrial employment, the inspector refused to impose a condition restricting change of use within Class B1 saying that the Use Classes Order seeks to afford flexibility to meet the changing needs of business and the economy and that such a condition would unnecessarily frustrate the aims of the Order.[20] In a further case involving Islington, the inspector refused to endorse the council's suggestion, that retention of light industrial floor space might be achieved by a section 52 agreement, on the basis that a condition to that effect would fail to accord with the spirit of the Use Classes Order.[21]

In a case involving premises in Hackney,[22] the inspector found that the council's aim to protect industrial uses conflicted with the Government's policy to permit a flexible approach whilst retaining effective control over changes of use that have a material impact in land use planning terms, on the local amenity or environment. In another appeal the inspector rejected a condition imposed on business premises in Covent Garden[23] that the premises should not be used as an office within the meaning of Sub-Class B1 (a) of the Use Classes Order. The inspector found that an office use would be likely to generate less rather than more traffic than an industrial use. There were other small office uses in the locality, but there was no evidence of substance that there was an over-provision of small office suites in the particular area or that such uses would be unacceptably harmful to the aims of the Covent Garden Action Area Plan. The distinction between office and light industrial uses no longer applies and development plan policies must be interpreted accordingly.[24] Various cases, mostly from London Boroughs concerned to keep their light industry base, in order, they believe, to generate employment, have confirmed the Government's insistence on this point.[25]

On an application to change the use of retail premises to independent offices in Tunbridge Wells, the council sought to limit application of Class B1 to offices and research and development, excluding industrial processes on the basis that the type of traffic likely to be generated was inappropriate. The inspector found in the local authority's favour because of the limited access. However, the council also considered that the application of Class A2 should be limited to professional services, excluding financial and other services, on the grounds of the likely generation of activity. The inspector found insufficient evidence of this and refused to impose the condition.[26]

In another case, light industrial uses were excluded by conditions imposed on Redditch premises, but seemingly without reasons being given.[27] In respect of premises at Reading, it was agreed to limit the type of office use to B1 offices to protect nearby residences.[28] But the inspector, when granting planning permission to convert stables to industrial and warehouse units, refused to impose a condition prohibiting office use.[29]

It is not only commercial uses which will not normally be restricted by condition. In a case involving a Class C2 use (residential institutions), the inspector refused to restrict the use to a residential care home even though such a condition would have been acceptable to the appellants.[30] However, a restriction has been imposed that if at any time a residential home for eight mentally handicapped children ceased to be used by the health authority for Class C2 purposes, planning permission would be required for any private continuance of that use.[31]

However there may be special circumstances which would justify a condition restricting the use of the site to particular uses in a Use Class. In an appeal involving premises in Teddington,[32] the inspector, if he had been minded to grant planning permission, said that he would have imposed a condition restricting the use to Sub-Class B1(c) (light industry) because the other sub-classes within B1 (offices and research and development) would generate a significantly larger car-parking requirement in a narrow street where parking was difficult. He also would have imposed a condition which required the council's approval for machinery to be installed even though a use within Class B1 could only be carried out in a residential area without detriment to its amenity. However, he rejected the appeal because the proposed building would be unduly dominant and overbearing in relation to the houses opposite.

The same argument surfaced in an appeal involving premises in Slough. It was said that the use of the premises should be restricted to a sub-class within Class B1 because other uses within the same class would generate too much parking.[33] In that case, the inspector gave consent for a general Class B1 use but imposed a condition to ensure that additional parking spaces were provided.

A case in Godalming[34] further illustrates that conditions may be imposed restricting uses within a Use Class for traffic reasons. In that case, the council's case was that the narrow width of the road giving access to the premises made it unsuitable for any traffic increase, particularly by goods vehicles. Larger goods vehicles could not enter and visibility from the access road was limited. The inspector found that there could be difficulties for larger goods vehicles attempting to enter or leave the site and that this could lead to the obstruction of the access road by manoeuvring vehicles with resulting delay and danger to other traffic, including pedestrians, and the detrimental effect of its appearance, noise and fumes on the dwellings in the conservation area. The inspector found that warehouse and industrial firms engaged in production were likely to have regular and frequent visits by larger goods vehicles for the delivery and collection of goods. Accordingly he imposed a condition excluding Sub-Class B1 (c) uses as well as storage and distribution uses within Class B8.

Restrictive conditions have been imposed on premises in the Peak Park[35] where the inspector was persuaded to grant planning permission for an extension and change of use of an agricultural building to light industrial use on land on a farm at Bradwell. The inspector found that there were exceptional circumstances which required special consideration owing to the creation of employment opportunities and the wide significance of technical developments. He imposed a condition that the building and extension should be used for the development, production and storage of extruded microwall plastic tubing and for no other purpose including Class B1 purposes. He also imposed a personal condition and a condition that the extension be removed on the use ceasing.

In a case of a mixed general and light industrial development at Newport[36] a condition has been imposed to prevent the development of part of the site for general industrial purposes because of the potential harmful effects of noise, smell and dust that such industry could have on the living environment of the existing residential occupiers and the future residents of a proposed housing estate.

However, conditions have been imposed which seek to ensure the industrial element of a mixed office and industrial development is used for that purpose. In a case in Southwark,[37] the inspector imposed a condition that the part of the development annotated as industrial floor space should be used for an industrial purpose and uses ancillary thereto and for no other purpose including any other purpose in Class B1 of the Order. The inspector found that there were exceptional circumstances to justify a condition limiting the use of the relevant parts to industrial use as the loss of industrial floor space would be likely to run contrary to the council's objectives of providing accommodation in the area giving a variety of employment opportunities.

Conditions have also been imposed restricting changes of use to uses within Class A2 (financial and professional services). In an appeal involving an application for a change of use of shop premises in Shepton Mallet[38] to estate agency use, the inspector accepted that an estate agency would give rise to visual interest to passers-by, not least because details of the property for sale would be constantly changing. Such visual interest may not hold good for other Class A2 uses, nor need they attract as many personal callers. The inspector therefore supported the need for the council's suggested conditions on maintaining a window display and restricting the change of use to estate agents only. The latter condition was justified as an exception to policy, even though the new Use Classes Order was acknowledged to provide for greater flexibility within the Financial and Professional Services Class. In a further case, involving premises at Sheringham,[39] the inspector attached a condition restricting the appeal premises to a building society use in order to preclude use for some alternative purposes under Class A2 of the Use Classes Order which might detract from the vitality of the centre. The inspector was satisfied that building societies provide an increasingly important range of facilities for the general public and that they should therefore be readily accessible to the local shopper. He was satisfied that the appeal proposals would make a positive contribution to the vitality of the Sheringham town centre, and that, having regard to the pattern of trade throughout the centre and preponderance of retail units in the immediate vicinity, the appeal site was a suitable location for the proposed use.

It may be questioned whether the conditions imposed restricting use rights could be justified in the last two cases. As Circular 13/87 acknowledges that service uses contribute to the vitality of shopping centres, it is doubtful how far it can be maintained that other uses within the Financial and Professional Services Class do not contribute to that vitality and should be excluded from the scope of a planning permission. In a case involving proposals for a betting shop in Basingstoke,[40] the inspector rejected the council's request to impose a condition that the premises should be used for a betting office only. He pointed out that government policy was to resist imposing conditions which had that limiting effect. He was not convinced that the peripheral location of the appeal premises justified such a condition based on the likelihood that there might be some activity in Class A2 which attracted far fewer callers than the betting shop and presented a much less interesting window display.

Restrictive conditions have been imposed to regulate uses within Class C2. A condition has also been attached on premises in Neath[41] that the premises should only be used as a nursing home or as a residential home for the elderly and for no other purpose including any other purpose within Class C2 of the Use Classes Order. The condition was imposed to maintain the sound residential character of the locality and adequate standards of road safety. As far as the latter reason is concerned, it was stated that less traffic would be generated if a building was to be used as a residential home for the elderly.

Circular 1/85 says that there may be occasional circumstances where a condition can be justified restricting changes of use so as to prevent the use of large retail premises as a food or convenience goods supermarket where such a use might generate an unacceptable level of additional traffic.[42] Such a condition effectively restricts the operator's rights under the Shops Class. In a case involving a DIY unit and garden centre,[43] the inspector imposed conditions to secure the satisfactory development of the site and to protect existing shopping centres and the amenities of adjoining residents. One of those conditions was to restrict the articles which could be sold to DIY goods, garden centre goods, furniture and carpets and for no other purpose within the Shops Class. In a case involving a non-food retail warehouse, a condition was imposed restricting the sales to furniture,[44] beds, carpets, floor coverings and ancillary electrical goods. In a further case involving a retail warehouse,[45] a condition was imposed that the retail units should only be used for the storage and sale of building and associated DIY products, flat-pack and general furniture, carpets and garden products and for no other purpose permitted under the Shops Class without the prior written agreement of the local planning authority. The condition was imposed to avoid the possible diversion of trade from established shopping centres with a consequent diminution in the quality and quantity of shopping in those centres. When the council agreed that the removal of such conditions would not harm the viability of any existing shopping centre, the inspector removed the conditions and accepted that they did not fit happily with national guidance on such matters.[46]

Subdivision

Subject to the terms of the Use Classes Order, the use of part of the land may be used for any purpose within the same Use Class as the rest of the land.[47] This means that subject to the terms of the Use Classes Order, land may be subdivided into separate units provided that their use remains within the same Use Class. This is a new provision which was brought into force in 1987 to overrule the effect of *Winton v S.O.S.E.*[48] which decided that on subdivision a material change in the use of part of the premises could occur even though both the existing and proposed uses fell within the same Use Class. The Government wanted to reverse the implication that where a person owned two industrial buildings on a site, he was unable to sell one for continued use for a similar industrial purpose within the same Use Class without obtaining planning permission.[49]

The Use Classes Order qualifies this provision only for dwellinghouses. The use as a separate dwelling-house of any part of the building or of any land occupied with and used for the same purposes as the building is not to be taken as not amounting to development.[50] This provision is necessary so that the Use Classes Order does not negate the effect of the provision which deems development occurs if a single dwelling-house is split into two or more separate dwelling-houses.[51]

One council sought to avoid the provision for subdivision by arguing that planning permission was required where, although the former and proposed uses were in the same Class C2, nevertheless, the proposed nursing home would have a lesser area and, therefore, the new use would not be in respect of the same planning unit as the former use. The inspector rejected this argument on the basis that, except as to a dwellinghouse, planning permission was not required for the subdivision of premises provided that both the existing and proposed uses fell within the same Use Class.[52]

Sui Generis Uses

There are many uses of land which are not included within any Use Class. Furthermore, some uses are specifically excluded from the operation of the Use Classes Order. These uses are often termed '*sui generis*' uses. At one time, the courts wished to interpret the Use Classes Order strictly so that other uses were not unwittingly embraced in its parameters. In *Tessier v S.O.S.E*,[53] Lord Widgery LCJ held that a sculptor's studio was not a general industrial building. He said that it was desirable that the Use Classes should not be stretched to embrace activities which clearly did not fall within them. However this dictum was not followed in *Forkhurst v S.O.S.E*.[54] in which Hodgson J said that Tessier's case was authority for the proposition that there could be a use which did not fall within any of the classes specified by the Secretary of State and to that extent it was undoubtedly right. In so far as it was persuasive authority for the proposition that the Use Classes should be interpreted restrictively rather than widely he did not agree with it and did not follow it.

The following uses are not included within any Use Class:

(a) as a theatre,
(b) as an amusement arcade or centre, or a funfair,
(c) for the washing or cleaning of clothes or fabrics in coin-operated machines or on premises at which the goods to be cleaned are received direct from the visiting public,
(d) for the sale of fuel for motor vehicles,
(e) for the sale or display for sale of motor vehicles,
(f) for a taxi business or business for the hire of motor vehicles,[55]
(g) as a scrapyard, or a yard for the storage or distribution of minerals or the breaking of motor vehicles.[56]

Circular 13/87 says that this list does not mean that such uses should always be regarded as environmentally undesirable and thus liable to be refused permission, but rather that in most places where such uses are proposed, consideration by local planning authorities will be justified.[57] The inclusion of amusement machines in premises used for other purposes does not necessarily bring those premises outside the scope of the Use Classes Order. Where a small number of amusement machines is installed in premises used for other purposes (for example, in cafés and hotels), it may be necessary to decide whether development is involved. Such uses may be ancillary to the primary use or insignificant in planning terms, in which case they will not need planning permission; this will depend on the facts.[58]

Unimplemented Permissions

The Use Classes Order applies where a building or other land is used for a purpose of any Use Class. Circular 13/87 points out that a use has to be implemented before the Order can have effect.[59] In many cases planning permission will be granted for use within a former Use Class such as light industry. The circular points out that it will still be necessary to apply for planning permission, for example, to use as offices a building with an extant but unimplemented light industrial permission. However, the possibility remains that if a building has been built as a light industrial building, it already should be considered as having a light industrial use when so adapted.[60] At some stage this point may need to be clarified by the courts. However, local planning authorities have been asked to take account of the spirit of the new Order in considering applications for a change of use of such buildings with an unimplemented use. They are also asked to do the same in respect of applications to remove conditions limiting the changes of use within one of the expanded classes.[61]

Hazardous Substances

No Use Class includes any use for a purpose which involves the manufacture, processing, keeping or use of a hazardous substance in such circumstances as will result in the presence at one time of a notifiable quantity of that substance in, on, over or under that building or land or any site of which that building or land forms part.[62] 'Hazardous substance' and 'notifiable quantity' have the meanings assigned to them by the Notification of Installations Handling Hazardous Substances Regulations 1982.[63] Those regulations contain a list of hazardous substances and the respective notifiable quantities. This restriction may have a severe influence on the effect of the Use Classes Order in individual cases. Time and effort may be spent trying to ascertain what substances were kept in a building before reliance is then placed on the Use Classes Order. When control over hazardous substances is introduced in a comprehensive manner,[64] the need to retain separate control in the Use Classes and General Development Orders can be relaxed.

References

1. Town and Country Planning Use Classes Order 1972 (SI No. 1385) amended by SI 1983 No. 1614.
2. Government White Paper: Lifting the Burden, Cmnd. 957, para. 3.1.
3. Town and Country Planning (Use Classes) Order 1987 (SI No. 764).
4. Circular 13/87, para. 3.
5. UCO 1987 Art. 3(3).
6. Circular 13/87, para. 8.

7. TCPA 1971, s.22(2)(f).
8. Ibid.: added by the Housing and Planning Act 1986, s.49, and Schedule 11, para. 1.
9. UCO 1987, Art. 3(2).
10. [1977] JPL 720 at p. 723.
11. [1984] JPL 809.
12. (1972) 23 P&CR 330.
13. *Rann v SSE* (1980) 40 P&CR 113.
14. *City of London Corporation v S.O.S.E.* (1971) 23 P&CR 169.
15. TCPA 1971, s.52.
16. TCPA 1971, s.32; see also ibid., s.31A.
17. Circular 13/87, paras. 11–12.
18. Spelthorne decision: T/APP/Z3635/A/86/53311/P3.
19. Kingston Upon Thames decision: T/APP/Z5630/A/87/75030/P4; see also Southall decision: T/APP/F5540/A/88/88517/P4.
20. Fulham Palace Road decision: T/APP/H5390/A/87/063254/P2.
21. Clerkenwell Green decision: T/APP/V5570/A/87/65532/P2.
22. T/APP/U5360/A/87/78728/P3.
23. T/APP/X5210/A/88/084805/P5.
24. Bracknell decision: T/APP/Co305/A/86/054256/P5.
25. Two Islington decisions: APP/V5570/A/87/082482/P3 and APP/V5570/A/88/083794; Camden decision: APP/X5210/A/88/086131; Hounslow decision: APP/F5540/A/88/091719; Southwark decision: T/APP/A5840/A/88/92869; Tower Hamlets decision: APP/E5900/A/88/092643; Hammersmith&Fulham decision: APP/H5390/A/88/092881.
26. APP/M2270/A/88/083996/P5.
27. T/APP/Q1825/A/87/79981/P5.
28. T/APP/Qo315/A/88/086027/P4.
29. [1989] JPL 49.
30. *Thanet DC* and *Hurley* (1988) 3 PAD 151.
31. *Rochester CC* and *Medway H. A.* (1988) 3 PAD 189.
32. T/APP/L5810/A/87/067522/P5.
33. T/APP/Vo320/A/87/067292/P5.
34. T/APP/R3650/A/86/056453/P5.
35. T/APP/L1046/A/87/071621/P2.
36. P34/609 (Welsh Office).
37. T/APP/A5840/A/87/068719/P2.
38. T/APP/Q3305/A/87/075807/P4.
39. T/APP/Y2620/A/87/076710/P4.
40. T/APP/H1705/A/87/066588/P4.
41. P83/304 (Welsh Office).
42. Circular 1/85, para. 68.
43. *Plymouth CC* and *Plymouth Park Estates* (1987) 2 PAD 66.
44. *Worcester CC* and *Frincon* (1987) 2 PAD 76; see also *Poundstretcher v SSE* [1989] JPL 90.
45. *Newbury DC* and *Ushers Brewery* (1988) 3 PAD 174.
46. [1988] JPL 653.
47. TCPA 1971, s.22(2)(f), as amended by the Housing and Planning Act 1986, s.49 and Schedule 11, para. 1.

48. [1984] JPL 188.
49. Circular 19/86, para. 9.
50. Town and Country Planning Use Classes Order ('UCO') 1987, para. 4; see also *Wakelin v SSE* (1983) 46 P&CR 214.
51. TCPA 1971, s.22(3)(a).
52. *Liverpool CC* and *Dr. K. R. Laghari* (1988) 3 PAD 198.
53. [1976] JPL 39.
54. [1982] JPL 448.
55. See *J. Toomey Motors and Inticab v Basildon DC* [1982] JPL 775.
56. UCO 1987, Art. 3(6).
57. Circular 13/87, para. 13.
58. DCPN No. 11 Annex, para. 7.
59. Circular 13/87, para. 11.
60. See, for example, *Backer v S.O.S.E.* (1984) 47 P&CR 149.
61. Circular 13/87, para 11.
62. UCO 1987, Art. 3(5).
63. 1982 S.I. No. 1357.
64. TCPA 1971, ss.58B–58N, introduced by the Housing and Planning Act 1986, s.31, but not yet brought into force.

6 SHOPPING AREA USES

In part A of the Use Classes Order there are three Use Classes which cover uses generally found in shopping areas. These are:

Class A1: Shops
Class A2: Financial and Professional Services
Class A3: Food and Drink

Provision is made for service uses by providing for new classes, one to cover financial and professional services and the other to cover food and drink. The new circular recognises that service uses, including fast-food restaurants, contribute to the vitality of shopping centres. In addition, fast-food restaurants often help to create employment opportunities, particularly for young people.[1]

Local planning authorities are advised not to use the new Use Classes to keep particular uses out of shopping areas. The new Financial and Professional Services Class means that permission for such uses may be given more readily as the new Order will not permit a subsequent change to offices with blank façades and not directly serving the public.[2]

Class A1 Shops

Class A1 covers use for all or any of the following purposes:

(a) for the retail sale of goods other than hot food,
(b) as a post office,
(c) for the sale of tickets or as a travel agency,
(d) for the sale of sandwiches or other cold food for consumption off the premises,
(e) for hairdressing,
(f) for the direction of funerals,
(g) for the display of goods for sale,
(h) for the hiring out of domestic or personal goods or articles,
(i) for the reception or service of goods to be washed, cleaned or repaired,

where the sale, display or service is to visiting members of the public.

It must be remembered that some uses are excluded from the effects of the Use Classes Order and therefore Class A1 will not cover them. In this connection, Class A1 will not cover such uses as an amusement arcade or centre or as a funfair, uses for the sale of fuel for motor vehicles, for the sale or display for sale of motor vehicles, for a taxi business or a business for the hire of motor vehicles (see above p.42).[3] Although dry cleaners may rely on the Use Class to open a shop for the reception or service of goods to be washed, cleaned or repaired, nevertheless such a use should not embrace a launderette or other establishment in which the washing or cleaning of clothes or fabrics takes place on the premises.[4]

This new class replaces Class I of the 1972 Order. Class I of the old Order covered use as a shop for any purpose except as a shop for the sale of hot food, a tripe shop, a shop for the sale of pet animals or birds, a cats-meat shop and a shop for the sale of motor vehicles. The 1972 Order defined shop as a building used for the carrying on of any retail trade or business wherein the primary purpose was the selling of goods by retail, and included a building for the purposes of a hairdresser, undertaker, travel agency, ticket agency or post office or for the reception of goods to be washed, cleaned or repaired or for any other purpose appropriate to a shopping area, but did not include a building used as a funfair, amusement arcade, pin-table saloon, garage, launderette, petrol-filling station, office, betting office, hotel, restaurant, snack-bar or café or premises licensed for the sale of intoxicating liquors for consumption on the premises.[5]

The new Order expressly includes sandwich bars (where food is consumed off the premises), showrooms (other than for motor vehicles) and hire shops. The exclusion of a snack bar from the definition of shop in the 1972 Order[6] may have meant that such shops were outside its scope. The circular reminds one that it is the primary purpose which should be considered: a sandwich bar does not cease to be in the Shops Class merely because it also sells hot drinks, or if a few customers eat on the premises.[7] In a case in Gray's Inn Road, Camden,[8] the inspector found that the primary use of the appeal premises was for the sale of cold food even though half the ground floor was used for seating. His conclusion provides a useful insight into how inspectors are likely to deal with such cases:

In acknowledging that half of the ground floor is available for seating, I am conscious of the stricture of para. 8 [of Circular 13/87] which indicates that consideration should be given to more than simply the amount of floor space occupied by different uses. On the evidence before me, it can reasonably be concluded that the primary use of the appeal premises is for the sale of cold food and from the survey information presented by far the greatest proportion of such cold food sales are consumed off the premises. Such hot food sales as take place including hot beverages, are but a small part of the total trade. Although some hot fillings are provided, this component forms the content of sandwiches or baps; this hot food does not form the foundation of a different type of meal such as might be associated with a restaurant. Such cooking as takes place in the basement in the early morning as preparation for fillings does not in my judgment undermine the primary nature of the premises which in my view derives from the counter service offering mainly cold food. Further, on the information before me whereby around 80 out of approaching 500 customers daily chose to avail themselves of the seating, I come to the view that such usage is well subordinated and incidental to the primary activity which is supplying sandwiches/baps and cold food for consumption off the premises and that it does not comprise a separate use sufficient to exclude the premises from sub-category (d).

Showrooms and hire shops may have been considered to be other purposes appropriate to a shopping area but the new Order makes it clear that they are included within the Shops Class. Similarly pet shops, catsmeat shops and tripe shops are now included within the Shops Class. Postal offices, but not postal sorting offices, are within the Shops Class.[9]

Class A2 Financial and Professional Services

Class A2 is the Financial and Professional Services Class. It covers use for the provision of:

(a) financial services
(b) professional services
(c) any other services (including use as a betting office) which it is appropriate to provide in a shopping area, where the services are provided principally to visiting members of the public.

Health and medical services are not included in this Use Class and are dealt with in Class D1.

The circular points out that banks and building society offices are now part of the established shopping scene. Other newer financial and professional services will need to be accommodated in shop-type premises. The new class will enable planning control to be maintained over proposals involving the conversion of shops for purposes other than for the retail sale of goods while permitting a free interchange within a wide range of service uses which the public now expects to find in shopping centres.[10]

Class II of the 1972 Order covered use for an office for any purpose. 'Office' was defined to include a bank and premises occupied by an estate agency, building society or employment agency or (for office purposes only) for the business of car hire or instruction but did not include a post office or betting office.[11] The old Class II has now been split so that uses more appropriate to a shopping area are covered by the new Class A2 while other uses are covered by the new Business Class B1.

The new class covers such uses as the branch of a bank, estate agency, employment agency and betting office. It will include an accountant's or solicitor's office where the services are provided principally to members of the public. The high street solicitor will be able to have the benefit of this Use Class but if his practice becomes more commercial and less dependent on visiting members of the public, then he may find that his use has drifted to that covered by the Business Class. It may be questioned whether there would be a material change of use if a solicitor's practice changed over the period of time from a high street practice to a commercial practice. Such a change may bring the use into the Business Class but it would not necessarily amount to a material change of use. If such a change was not considered material, Class B1 could be introduced into the high street by the back door without the formal need for planning permission.

Not all bank premises will now fall within Class A2. The head offices and other purely administrative offices will find themselves in the new Business Class. An over-the-counter insurance service behind a display window without prior appointment and without an extensive on-the-spot administrative back-up has been held to fall within Class A2.[12]

Excluded from the operation of the Order are taxi businesses and car hire businesses. However, driving instruction offices have not been specifically excluded and may fall within this Use Class.

To change a retail shop into a service outlet within Class A2 will normally involve development. Advice on the acceptability of such a proposal can be found in Development Control Policy Note No. 11 – Service Uses in Shopping Areas. The Note points out[13] that the impact of a dead frontage can be avoided or reduced by the dispersal of non-retail uses within a shopping centre. Where change to non-retail use is permitted, it may be appropriate to do so subject to a condition requiring the provision of a window display, but such a condition should only be imposed where it can be justified.

Class A3 Food and Drink

Class A3 covers use for the sale of food and drink for consumption on the premises or of hot food for consumption off the premises. This class will include hot food shops, restaurants, cafés, snack bars, wine bars and public houses. Circular 13/87 explains the reasoning for the new class:

> The new class reflects the breaking down of the traditional boundaries between different types of premises. It will enable the catering trade to adapt to changing trends and demands with greater speed and certainty in premises where the potential environmental nuisances such

as smell, traffic and parking have already been accepted. Local planning authorities should continue to treat planning applications for new premises falling within this class on their merits in the light of the general presumption in favour of development. Granting permission subject to conditions designed to alleviate a particular difficulty should always be considered as an alternative to refusal where serious environmental problems are envisaged.[14]

The new Class A3 embraces a wide spectrum. A café can now be used for a hot food take-away shop even if there had been a previous enforcement notice against the latter use.[15]

Attempts to restrict uses strictly to those demised in the Class A3 may not succeed. In a recent case, the local authority sought to enforce against use of a public house as a 'theme' pub with ancillary entertainment in the form of darts, skittles, pool tables, amusement machines and amplified loud music. A condition had been imposed that the premises should not be used for any other purpose than as a public house and licensed restaurant. However the inspector rejected the attempt to enforce against the ancillary facilities:

It remains for me to consider whether the manner in which Ocean 11 is run falls within the definition 'public house and licensed restaurant' as required by the condition. At the inquiry, it was accepted that there is no official definition of a public house other than the generally held view that it is an establishment where the main source of income is derived from the sale of intoxicating liquor for consumption by customers on the premises. In that 70 per cent of the income of Ocean 11 comes from that source, it satisfies the generally held view that it is a public house. As the evidence given has shown, there have always been ancillary activities in public houses to attract custom. Over the years, the form of these activities has changed. The latest change involves the establishment of 'theme', 'fun' and 'disco' pubs where admission charges are often raised to cover the cost of entertainment. These establishments are however still regarded as public houses. This is the case with Ocean 11 where, in addition to the musical entertainment, food and drink are available. While this may well be a different form of public house from that of bygone days and may well not have been the type of facility intended by the Council when they granted planning permission in 1985, I do not find any restriction in the condition then applied which precludes the establishment of a 'theme' pub.

I can well appreciate the concern of local residents at the disturbance which occurs when clientele from Ocean 11 leave the premises in the early hours of the morning. Opening hours of such an establishment are however a matter for Licensing Justices. Moreover, it is a further fact that the behaviour of the public outside licensed premises such as Ocean 11 is a matter which cannot properly be regulated by planning control.[16]

An application for change of use of a retail shop to a Class A3 use will often involve amenity issues. Problems about smell and litter arising from hot food shops are addressed in Development Control Policy Note No. 11 on Service Uses in Shopping Areas. The Note says that problems of smell and litter may mean a substantial loss of amenity or have a detrimental effect on the character of an area, and are perhaps most likely to be an issue affecting proposals for hot food shops. As they are subject to other statutory controls these matters should not be accorded undue weight in planning decisions. Such problems too can sometimes be alienated by conditions.[17] Conditions on hours of use may be imposed to control noise particularly in residential areas.[18]

References

1. Circular 13/87, para. 15.
2. Circular 13/87, para. 16.
3. UCO 1987, Art. 3(6).
4. UCO 1987, Art. 3(6)(c).
5. UCO 1972, Art. 2(2). The definition of 'shop' also differs in the Shop Act 1950, regulating Sunday trading: *Erewash BC v Ilkeston Consumer Co-operative Society Ltd.* [1988] EGCS 103.
6. UCO 1972, Art. 2(2).
7. Circular 13/87, para. 17.
8. [1988] JPL 137.
9. Circular 13/87, para. 17.
10. Circular 13/87, para. 18.
11. UCO 1972, Art. 2(2).
12. *Oxford CC* and *Endsleigh Insurance* (1988) 3 PAD 73.
13. Development Control Policy Note ('DCPN'), No. 11, para. 14. This Note has not been updated in the light of the Use Classes Order.
14. Circular 13/87, para. 19.
15. T/APP/U4610/A/86/61121/P4. See also *City of Aberdeen v SSS* [1987] JPL 292, in which it was held that there was no change of use from a counter-service restaurant to a hot food take-away service under the Town and Country Planning (Use Classes) (Scotland) Order 1973. For the effect of an enforcement notice on other uses, see *St. Herman's Estate Co. Ltd. v Havant and Waterloo UDC* (1971) 69 LGR 286 and TCPA 1971, s.93.
16. *Shepway DC* and *South Coast Leisure* (1988) 3 PAD 178; see also *Exeter CC* and *Dow* and *Chan* (1989) 4 PAD 75.
17. DCPN No. 11, para. 24; see also Annex, paras. 15–18.
18. DCPN No. 11, para. 18.

7 OTHER BUSINESS AND INDUSTRIAL USES

Part B of the new Business Class contains these Use Classes:

Class B1: Business
Class B2: General Industrial
Classes B3–7: Special Industrial
Class B8: Storage and Distribution

It is provided that where land on a single site or on adjacent sites as parts of a single undertaking is used for purposes consisting of or including purposes falling within any two or more classes of B1–B7, those classes may be treated as a single class in considering the use of the land, so long as the area used for a purpose falling either within the General Industrial B2 Class or the Special Industrial Classes B3–B7 is not substantially increased as a result.[1]

Class B1 Business

Class B1 covers use for the following purposes:

(a) as an office other than a use falling within Class A2 (Financial and Professional Services),
(b) for research and development of products or processes, or
(c) for any industrial process,
being a use which can be carried out in any residential area without detriment to the amenity of that area by reason of noise, vibration, smell, fumes, smoke, soot, ash, dust or grit.

The new class amalgamates the former office Class II with the former light industrial Class III but excludes the uses falling within the new Financial and Professional Class A2. Provided that the limitation specified in the class is satisfied, this class will also include other laboratories and studios and 'high-tech' uses, spanning office, light industrial and research and development (for example, the manufacture of computer hardware and software, computer research and development, provision of consultancy services and after-sales services, as well as micro-engineering, biotechnology and pharmaceutical research, development and manufacture, in either offices or light industrial premises, whichever are more suitable).[2] The new definition of 'industrial process' means that film, video or sound recording can now be carried on within this Use Class.[3]

There are two limitations to the new Use Class. Firstly, uses falling within the Financial and Professional Service Uses Class A2 are excluded. Whether or not such a service would fall in that Use Class will depend on whether the services provided are principally to visiting members of the public. A high street solicitor's office is, therefore, likely to fall within Class A2 but a commercial solicitor's office will fall in this Class B1. The main purpose of the use must be considered in this context because many solicitors' offices will deal with commercial cases as well as providing services to visiting members of the public. Similarly, the high street branch of a bank will fall within Class A2 but the head office or purely administrative offices will fall within Class B1. In practice, this distinction will mean that many offices will find themselves excluded from Class B1.

The second limitation is that the use must be capable of being carried out in any residential area without detriment to the amenity of that area by reason of noise, vibration, smell, fumes, smoke, soot, ash, dust or grit. This test is hypothetical as there does not need to be an actual residential area in the vicinity. The 1972 Order had a limitation on light industrial use by applying the test to the processes to be carried on or the machinery to be installed.[4] In the new Order, all aspects of the use have to be considered.[5] It is significant, though, that traffic generation has not been specifically included within the test. However, since all aspects of the use fall to be considered, it has been interpreted to include noise and vibration arising from traffic generated by the use.[6] The circular advises that there will normally be no material changes of use requiring planning permission until an intensification or change in the nature of the use is such that the use would no longer satisfy the limitation specified in the class.[7] The test is whether the use can be carried out in any residential area without detriment to the amenity of that area. It is not whether it can be carried out in a particular area. In *W. T. Lamb v SSE*,[8] the Secretary of State was upheld in his view that the test could not be satisfied even though the premises were in proximity to Gatwick Airport. One council, Spelthorne BC, considered[9] that the second limitation reduced the degree to which offices and light industry fall within the Use Class's ambit. Thus, it concluded, in considering 'all aspects of the use', that only small-scale uses, 235 m^2 or less, should be included, on traffic noise grounds alone. Most cases over 235 m^2 would not be determined by the council because they would fall outside Class B1 owing to noise resulting from traffic generation. This policy has been appealed.[10]

A light industrial use must involve an 'industrial process'. The definition of an 'industrial process' is considered in the next section.

Rather surprisingly, the main accommodation used by local authorities may not fall either in Class B1 or even in Class A2. In the case of the County Hall complex (formerly the council offices of the Greater London

Council), the Secretary of State found that the primary use of the building was for the exercise of local government statutory functions. The characteristics of these functions were sufficiently different from commercial office use to support the conclusion that the use of the planning unit should be regarded as *sui generis*.[11] His conclusion in this respect has been supported by the High Court. It was held that the complex had a London governmental use which was a distinctive use not able to be described as an office use as the office activity was merely incidental to this other use.[12] The rider at the end of the decision by the Secretary of State should be noted: the decision was made on the special facts of the particular case, and a different conclusion might be reached regarding the use of local government buildings in different circumstances.[13]

Class B2 General Industrial

Class B2 covers general industrial use and is defined as a use for the carrying on of an industrial process other than one falling within the Business Class B1 or the Special Industrial Classes B3–B7. In effect it is the same class as Class IV in the Use Classes Order 1972 save that it is not limited to land containing a building.

The definition of 'industrial process' is appropriate for all the Classes within Part B but it will be convenient to deal with the definition here. 'Industrial process' means a process for or incidental to any of the following purposes:

(a) the making of any article or part of any article (including a ship or vessel, or a film video or sound recording);
(b) the altering, repairing, maintaining, ornamenting, finishing, cleaning, washing, packing, canning and adapting for sale, breaking up or demolition of any article; or
(c) the getting, dressing or treatment of minerals;
in the course of any trade or business other than agriculture, and other than a use carried on in or adjacent to a mine or quarry.[14]

Although the definition now includes film, video or sound recording, these uses are likely to fall within Class B1 (see above, p. 52).

The process must be carried on in the course of any trade or business other than agriculture. However, neither the making of profit nor any commercial activity was an essential feature of a process 'carried on in the course of trade or business'. In *Rael-Brook v Minister of Housing and Local Government*,[15] the activity of a local authority in a building used as a cooking centre to provide school meals was held to be an industrial activity falling within the former Class III.

The process may be connected with another use in nearby premises and still remain an industrial activity within a Use Class. In *Horwitz v Rowson*[16] the storing and grading of bulbs and the making and repairing of boxes were held to be industrial processes even though they were in connection with the retail use of the shop on the other side of the road and no machinery other than a handsaw was used for those purposes.

It has been held that the use of land for car and heavy vehicle breaking is a general industrial use. The use of land for the storage of builders' equipment may amount to an industrial use where machinery is used to refurbish and renovate scaffolding.[17] The use of premises as a repair garage for motor cars on a commercial basis may amount to an industrial use but the use of premises for the purposes of a coach and bus business did not fall within any of the Use Classes.[18] Similarly, it has been held that a sculptor's studio or workshop does not fall within any of the industrial classes in the Use Classes Order and is a *sui generis* use.[19] The proposition in the sculptor's studio case that the scope of Use Classes should be interpreted restrictively rather than widely has not been followed.[20]

Classes B3–B7 Special Industrial

The Special Industrial Classes contain uses which potentially cause environmental detriment and are singled out for special treatment. The classes were formerly Classes V-IX of the 1972 Order. They are now the subject of review which may lead to some amendments being made. Despite the nature of a Special Industrial Use, planning permission may still be given for such a use to take place on an industrial estate especially if conditions could ensure compatibility with other uses.[21]

Class B4 includes recovering metal from scrap under Special Industrial Group B. This use is to be distinguished from use of a scrap yard which is *sui generis*, even though there are similarities between the two uses in that disused equipment and machinery is brought to the site, there are sorting and grading operations carried out and disposal is organised. The industrial process involved and the limitation to non-ferrous metal differentiated the use from that of a scrap yard where all forms of scrap are handled.[22]

Class B6 deals with Special Industrial Group D which includes producing or using cellulose or other pressure sprayed metal finishes (other than in vehicle repair workshops in connection with minor repairs, or the application of plastic powder by the use of fluidised bed and electrostatic spray techniques). In an enforcement notice appeal involving industrial premises in Worthing,[23] the appellant sought to argue that the paint spraying activity was ancillary to the general industrial use carried out. The inspector rejected that proposition holding that the paint spraying went beyond that which could be described as minor in nature and introduced another use to the premises which fell within Class B6 giving rise to a mixed use of the premises. Similarly there was a material change of use from use for coach-building, falling in the General Industrial Use Class, and use for the repair of motor vehicles with an emphasis on metal-work involving spraying with cellulose paint as part of the normal operations.[24]

Class B8 Storage or Distribution

Class B8 covers use as a storage or distribution centre. It is intended that it should remain the same as the former class which covered use as a wholesale warehouse or repository for any purpose. The new description was to make it clear that retail warehouses – where the main purpose is the sale of goods direct to visiting members of the public – will generally fall within the Shops Class however much floor space is used for storage. The use may now attach to land as well as to a building.

The former description 'wholesale warehouse or repository' gave rise to attempts to turn warehouses into shops under the guise of the Use Classes Order. These attempts did not find favour with the Secretary of State who was supported by the courts. In 1971, he issued an appeal decision defining 'wholesale warehouse' to exclude the selling of goods to the public in larger quantities than are normal in a retail shop or at a discount which would not bring such sales within the term 'wholesale'.[25]

In *Calcaria Construction Co. v S.O.S.E.*, the judge said that a 'warehouse is not a "shop" despite the attempts of various traders to call their shops "discount warehouses".' Planning permission for the erection of a warehouse for wholesale and retail distribution of foodstuffs and household goods did not enable a supermarket of 40,000 sq. ft. (3,715 m²) to be built. The word 'warehouse' is used where the main function of the building is intended to be for storage and distribution from the building.[26]

In *L.T.S.S. Print and Supply Services v Hackney LBC*,[27] the Court of Appeal upheld the Secretary of State's view that a 'cash and carry warehouse' was not a wholesale warehouse. The Secretary of State accepted that the business of warehousing may contain a wholesale sales element, but for the use of the building for such sales to be permitted, these sales must be ancillary to the use of the building as a warehouse.

A further attempt was later made to argue that a 'Do-It-Yourself supermarket' could take place in premises approved as general warehousing units and builders' merchants' warehouse. Lord Widgery LCJ, in *Monomart (Warehouses) Ltd v S.O.S.E.*,[28] said that a 'warehouse' has a very well-known meaning in ordinary English. It is a place where goods are stored preparatory to their being taken elsewhere and sold. A warehouse is not a place where retail sales are carried out and, at all events, not where retail sales are the principal activity within the building. A warehouse for builders' supplies does not include the sale of builders' supplies by retail as a principal activity on the premises.

It is not necessary that the storage should be as part of a business. In *Newbury DC v S.O.S.E.*,[29] the House of Lords held that the word 'repository for any purpose' in the Use Classes Order 1950 covered the use of hangars by the Home Office for the storage of fire pumps and equipment vehicles. There was no justification for implying a requirement that a repository should be a place where goods are stored as part of a storage business or that the storage should be in the course of a trade or business at all.

Within Class B8, there may be uses which are ancillary to the main use as a storage or distribution centre. In one case, the Secretary of State determined that the use of premises for grading, boxing, storage and distribution of fish would not constitute or involve development of land even though the sorting and re-packing might have been considered light industrial if not ancillary to the main use.[30]

References

 1. UCO 1987, Art. 3(4).
 2. Circular 13/87, para. 20.
 3. UCO 1987, Art. 2.
 4. UCO 1972, Art. 2(2): definition of 'light industrial building'.
 5. Circular 13/87, para 21.
 6. Teddington case: T/APP/L5810/A/87/067522/P5.
 7. Circular 13/87, para. 21.
 8. [1983] JPL 303; see also *Essex CC v SSE* [1974] JPL 286.
 9. Spelthorne Borough Council Interim Policy Note concerning Use Class B1–Business.
10. Robinson and Pursar, 'The B1 shuffle', *Estates Gazette*, 3 December 1988.
11. [1988] JPL 193.
12. *London Residuary Body v SSE* [1988] 2 PLR 79. This decision is difficult to reconcile with *Shephard v Buckinghamshire County Council* (1967) 18 P&CR 419, in which office and administrative functions connected with military purposes were held to be offices falling in Class II of UCO 1963. In *Westminster City Council v British Waterways Board* (1985) 49 P&CR 117, the House of Lords rejected the proposition that the established use of premises was a street cleaning depot: such a use was only one of a substantial range of uses which could properly be carried out without involving a material change of use. The House of Lords rejected the contention that the use was ancillary to activities carried on outside the premises.
13. [1988] JPL 193.
14. UCO 1987, Art. 2.
15. (1967) 18 P&CR 290.
16. [1960] 1 WLR 803.
17. *Forkhurst v SSE and Brentwood DC* [1982] JPL 448.

18. *Day & Mid-Warwickshire Motors Ltd. v SSE and Solihull MDC* [1979] JPL 538.
19. *Tessier v SSE* (1976) 31 P&CR 161.
20. *Forkhurst v SSE and Brentwood DC* [1982] JPL 448.
21. *Richmondshire DC* and *Markendale – Lancashire* (1986) 1 PAD 131.
22. [1989] JPL 130.
23. T/APP/M3835/C86/4039/P6.
24. *Scrivener v MHLG* (1967) 18 P&CR 357.
25. This decision was quoted in Development Control Policy Note 14 – Warehouses – Wholesale, Cash and Carry, etc. (now cancelled).
26. (1974) 27 P&CR 435.
27. (1976) 31 P&CR 133: see also *Cambridge CC* and *Hadjioannou* (1986) 1 PAD 256.
28. (1977) 34 P&CR 305.
29. (1980) 40 P&CR 148.
30. *Colchester BC* and *Craven and Seeley* (1987) 2 PAD 389.

8 RESIDENTIAL USES

The new Use Classes Order has three Use Classes to deal with residential uses:

Class C1: Hotels and hostels
Class C2: Residential institutions
Class C3: Dwelling-houses

Class C1 Hotels and Hostels

Class C1 covers use as a hotel, boarding or guest house or as a hostel where, in each case, no significant element of care is provided. 'Care' in this context means 'personal care for people in need of such care by reason of old age, disablement, past or present dependence on alcohol or drugs or past or present mental disorder'.[1] So that hostels where no significant element of care is provided are now to be treated akin to boarding houses.[2] In this respect, the new Order departs from general planning law by providing that the identity of the user or the type of person to be accommodated by reference to age or other characteristics becomes a land use planning consideration.[3]

Class XI of the 1972 Order covered use of a boarding or guest house, or a hotel providing sleeping accommodation. However, hostels were excluded from the previous Class XI, while use of a building as a 'students' hostel' was held to be *sui generis* so as also not to fall within the former Class XI.[4] A hostel has been described by Glidewell J as follows:

> ... in modern English usage, it meant a building in which people either lived or stayed which provided communal facilities. The sleeping accommodation was often, although not by any means always, in dormitories rather than single rooms and provided shared cooking, eating and recreational facilities. It was of the essence of a hostel that its accommodation was relatively basic and inexpensive, but in any sense the word was not a term of art in relation to the duration of the stay. It embraced institutions – if that was a correct categorisation – which covered the whole range from long-term accommodation, as for instance a students' hostel or a nurses' hostel where one normally would have expected that people were staying at least for a term, often for a year at a time or more, to, for instance, a youth hostel which by

definition was occupied by transients – people who were staying for a day or two at the most.[5]

One source of planning appeals has been the change of use to a hostel for homeless persons run by local authorities often in the areas of other local authorities, thus giving rise to enforcement action. In *Panayi v SSE*,[6] Kennedy J upheld the inspector's description of premises being used as a hostel where four self-contained flats were being used to provide accommodation for homeless families placed there by another London borough.

The question arises as to what uses will fall within the new Use Class embracing hostels as well as hotels and boarding houses. In *Birmingham Corporation v Habib Ullah*,[7] the Divisional Court held that a change of a private dwelling-house to that of a house used for multiple paying occupation could amount to a material change of use. In *Breachberry v SSE*,[8] multiple occupation provided by the DHSS was held not to fall within the former Class XI. Although such uses could now be argued to be hostel uses and so fall within the new Class C1, the circular advises that multiple occupation will generally fall outside the terms of the Order.[9] In *Mayflower Cambridge v SSE*,[10] the Divisional Court upheld a distinction being drawn between a building used for bed-sitting rooms and a building used as a hotel on the basis that a hotel implied that the accommodation was transitory. The use of premises as bed-sitting rooms would normally be considered a form of multiple occupation, although, in some circumstances the use could be considered as a hostel use falling within Class C1. (Use of only part of a dwelling-house as a bed-sitter would not take the premises outside Class C3 (dwelling-houses) if the character and use of the building remained essentially residential.) Use as a residential club would still be likely to be outside the new Use Class.[11]

A hotel should normally cater for transient guests. In the following passage, Lord Widgery LCJ sought to describe a hotel use:[12]

> Essentially, of course, it is the short lets which produced the hotel use in this case, but it is not short lets as such which must necessarily in all cases be proved. Nor is it necessary, to establish a hotel use, to prove that meals are being offered or that there are a number of porters or kitchen maids which a hotel use may require. If one has the transient population, the constant change in the identity of people present, the fact that such a use requires generally the presence of a restaurant and more porters is merely indicative of the fact that it is a different sort of use. One does not have to prove that in order to say that the use is a use as a hotel.

It is doubtful whether this passage can be justified in excluding residential hotels from the definition of 'hotel' where the usual characteristics of a hotel are present but the guests stay on a longer term basis.

Class C2 Residential Institutions

Class C2 covers residential institutions which include uses:

> for the provision of residential accommodation and care to people in need of care (other than dwelling-houses);
> as a hospital or nursing home;
> as a residential school, college or training centre.

The characteristic of this Use Class is, apart from educational establish-, ments, the provision of personal care and treatment (distinguishing the class from the Hotels and Hostels Class) and the fact that the residents and staff do not form a single household (distinguishing the class from dwelling-houses).[13]

For this class, care means personal care for people in need of such care by reason of old age, disablement, past or present dependence on alcohol or drugs or past or present mental disorder and includes the personal care of children and medical care and treatment.[14] Hostels where care is provided should be treated as residential care homes.[15]

This class combines Classes XII and XIV of the 1972 Order. Class XII covered use as a residential or boarding school or a residential college. Class XIV covered used as a home or institution providing for the boarding, care and maintenance of children, old people or persons under disability, a convalescent home, a nursing home, a sanatorium or a hospital. In *Rann v SSE*,[16] it was held that a holiday home used in the summer for mentally handicapped persons did not fall within Class XIV owing to the transitory nature of the stay of each visitor. The need for care and maintenance implied that one would have expected a matron to be employed in the home. Whether the same use would now fall within Class C1 or Class C2 would mainly depend on whether a *significant* element of care was provided.

The circular addresses the point that residential care homes and nursing homes may place additional demands on already stretched essential services. Government advice is that it is important for local planning authorities to concentrate on the land use planning considerations to be taken into account when considering a planning application for a change of use to a use falling within this class. They will need to concern themselves mainly with the impact of a proposed institution on amenity and the environment. They should avoid giving the impression that if planning permission is granted the necessary registration is likely to follow automatically. Unless the institution is managed or provided by a body constituted by an Act of Parliament or incorporated by Royal Charter, all private and voluntary homes (except residential care homes with three beds or less) have to be registered with the local social services authority or the district health authority. Registration can be refused on the grounds that the home would not provide adequate services or facilities reasonably required by residents or patients. The registering authorities may consult each other and the family practitioner committee about the provision of health and social services for residents.[17]

In a recent case, the inspector allowed a change of use from a dwelling-house to a residential institution even though the local planning authority pointed out (but did not support in evidence) that there was a serious population imbalance in the district and that more old people would put a strain on medical services and adversely affect the reputation of the district as a prime holiday area. The fact that there were no amenity or environmental objections was a decisive factor.[18]

In another case involving an application to erect a twelve bed-space shared housing project for the mentally ill, the inspector said that it could not be right that planning permission for an identical building could be granted for another C2 use (e.g. a residential institution for the elderly) which would probably not be objected to locally, but could be withheld for a similar proposal for mentally ill patients. The natural fears and anxiety of local residents, particularly regarding possible dangers posed by residents, were probably unfounded. Even if soundly based, such fears could not be regarded as overriding land use planning matters. The legitimate planning concerns regarding amenity should be based on physical factors such as overlooking, overshadowing or undue noise disturbance, rather than on psychological factors.[19]

Some local planning authorities have policies seeking to support hotel uses in tourist areas. These policies can affect decisions relating to changes of use of hotels to Class C2 uses. For example, a hotel in Blackpool was situated in a prime holiday area on a non-statutory plan. The inspector refused to allow a change of use of the hotel to a single rest home. While such a proposal in itself would not have a very serious effect on the character of a relatively quiet frontage, a proliferation of such uses would certainly produce a marked change. He thought that if the appeal was allowed, further applications in respect of other premises along the frontage would follow inevitably and individually, and such applications would be difficult to resist.[20] A case in Criccieth raised a similar concern. However, bearing in mind the number of empty hotel bed spaces in the town in recent years, the inspector was satisfied that the change of use applied for would not cause demonstrable harm to the character or tourist industry of Criccieth. He therefore allowed the appeal to change the use of a hotel to a residential home for the mentally ill.[21] In a further case the inspector allowed the appeal for a Class C2 use because the appeal site in St. Ives was not a prime hotel area so that the local policy did not apply.[22]

Class C3 Dwelling-houses

For the first time, the Use Classes Order now has a Use Class reserved for dwelling-houses. Class C3 covers use as a dwelling-house (whether or not as a sole or main residence):

(a) by a single person or by people living together as a family, or
(b) by not more than six residents living together as a single household (including a household where care is provided for residents). [Care has the same meaning as in Class C1.]

It is now clear that a second holiday or weekend home may be used as such without the need for planning permission. However, it seems that a condition may be validly imposed that the accommodation can only be used as a unit of holiday accommodation.[23] However, it is not clear whether a holiday cottage being let out to a number of different families would fall within the Use Class. In *Blackpool BC v SSE*[24] where a house was let to a number of people over the summer months, the inspector's decision that the house was still being used as a private dwelling-house was accepted. It is doubtful whether such a use would fall within Class C3 as the premises are not being occupied by a single person or by people living together as a family but by a series of families one after the other. However, even if that use did not fall within Class C3, there may still not be a material change of use between a private dwelling-house and family holiday accommodation.

The key element in the use of a dwelling-house for other than family purposes is the concept of a single household. In the case of small residential care homes or nursing homes, staff and residents will probably not live as a single household and the use will therefore fall into the Residential Institutions Class, regardless of the size of the home. The single household concept will provide more certainty over the planning permission of small group homes which are said to play a major role in the government's community care policy which is aimed at enabling disabled and mentally disordered people to live as normal lives as possible in touch with the community. Any resident care staff should be included in the calculation of the number of people accommodated.[25]

The class includes not only families or people living together under arrangements for providing care and support within the community, but also other groups of people such as students, not necessarily related to each other, who choose to live on a communal basis as a single household. Most sheltered housing developments will fall within this class because they normally comprise a group of individual dwelling-houses. The use of a dwelling-house for other forms of multiple occupation will generally remain outside the scope of the Order.[26]

A case involving residential premises at Oldmixon[27] provides an insight into what is embraced by the requirement that not more than six residents must live together as a single household. In that case, it was proposed to use residential premises to house persons previously treated for alcohol and drug abuse at a nearby institution. After their stay, the residents would be expected to return to their normal life. The inspector found that the proposed use fell within Class C3:

> The distinction between Class C3(b) of the 1987 Order and Class C2 residential institutions, is the use of a dwelling house by not more than 6 residents living together as a single household. There is no disagreement between the parties that the appeal premises are a dwelling house or that the proposal meets the requirements for the number of persons to be accommodated. The main difference between them is whether the residents would form a single household. However I was told that it was an important feature of the proposed rehabilitation programme that they did. They would occupy the premises, without any resident staff; they would organise and share household duties such as cooking, washing and share the communal facilities of the premises; they would live as independently as possible from the Lodge developing social contacts, interests and voluntary activities in the general community. Whilst property and grounds maintenance would be provided by the Lodge I do not regard this as militating against the concept of a single household, as it is a feature of many family dwellings as well. Each resident would, I was told, be expected to stay for an average of 15 to 18 months and I agree that this is more than sufficient time for the formation of a single household. Most residents would live together for many months and thus have time to develop not only strong ties within the household but hopefully with local family residents as well. Whilst residents would probably stay for slightly different periods, joining and leaving the household at different times, this is not dissimilar to the pattern in student and other single households, which the Council and Circular 13/87 accept are included in Class C3(b). It is certainly very far removed from the circumstances of the case cited by the Council, where up to 75 persons occupied the premises, arriving without notice, staying for periods as short as a night or a week, some sleeping and eating to a rota.

The case cited by the council concerned a house run by Chiswick Women's Aid as a hostel for temporary accommodation of ill-treated women and their children where up to seventy-five persons resided at any one time. The House of Lords rejected the contention that the occupants could be described as members of a single household. Lord Hailsham gave his reasoning that no single household was present:[28]

> The *Oxford English Dictionary* [on 'household'] . . . gives: 'The inmates of a house collectively; an organised family, including servants or attendants dwelling in a house; a domestic establishment.' This gives some colour to the appellant's case. The trouble is that the first part of the definition would cover the inmates of any house and deprive the section of any meaning at all. . . . Both the expression 'household' and membership of it are questions of fact and degree, there being no certain *indicia* the presence or absence of any of which is by itself conclusive. In this case I am driven by at least three factors to place what happened in 369, Chiswick High Road, outside the limits of what can be conclusively called a single household. The first is the mere size. There comes a point at which all differences of degree becomes differences of kind. Neither 36 nor 75 is a number which in the suburbs of London as they exist at the present time can ordinarily and reasonably be regarded as a single household. The second factor is the fluctuating character of the resident population both as regards the fact of fluctuation and the extent of it. The residents were coming and going in the words of Lord Widgery C.J. 'each day or each week'. The first of the Canadian cases cited above does attempt a definition which, I think rightly, implies something more durable and more intimate than the fortuitous relationship between the unhappy inmates of no. 369 at the material times. The third consideration is the fact that I cannot regard a temporary place of refuge for fortuitous arrivals as ordinarily forming a household at all. These residents came from a variety of homes and may have gone to a variety of different places after leaving no. 369. No doubt some would have gone back home. These would never have ceased to be members of their former household. Others will have gone to relatives. Others will have been found accommodation elsewhere. They never had the intention to use no. 369 as more than a temporary harbour in a storm. Whilst they were in no. 369 no doubt each looked after her own children where possible, and no doubt each conformed with the very reasonable communal organisation described in the stated case. I do not think that every community consisting of temporary migrants housed under a single roof reasonably organised constitutes or can constitute a single household. I do not think that this is necessarily true of a hostel, a monastery or a school, but it is certainly not true of a temporary haven in a storm.

A question which is often asked is how far a business may be operated from home. The question that may now be asked is whether business use from home takes the use of the premises outside Class C3. Government advice is that permission for working at home is not usually needed where the use of part of a dwelling-house for business purposes does not change the overall character of its use as a residence.[29] Circular 2/86 stresses that the use by the householder of a room as an office would not normally require permission.

Many small businesses are started by people working in their own homes. This will not necessarily require planning permission. It should not be assumed as a matter of course that such use of part of the dwelling-house necessarily involves a material change of use requiring permission. That is unlikely to be involved where the use of part of a dwelling-house for business purposes does not change the overall character of its use as a residence. For example, the use by the householder of a room as an office would not normally require permission. Even where new activities constitute a separate use within the planning unit, the new use may be de minimis in planning terms. On the other hand, the scale of business use may be significant enough to alter the overall residential character of the dwelling-house. This would constitute a material change of use for which planning permission will be required.[30]

The Planning Policy Guidance Note on Industrial and Commercial Development and Small Firms goes on to point out that it is reasonable that where business use becomes dominant or intrusive, permission should be required (and may be refused), but many small businesses may be carried on from home without any serious detriment to neighbouring property.[31] The Department of the Environment booklet 'A Step by Step Guide to Planning Permission for Small Businesses' gives more detailed advice by means of a table (see facing page). The table stresses that the question is whether the character and use of the building remain essentially residential.

There has been a tendency to find that the use of a small part of a premises as a doctor's surgery does not involve a material change of use.[32] Use of one ground-floor room for chiropody has been stated not to involve development.[33] In each case, the question is one of fact and degree. Where the ancillary activity is damaging to amenity, there is likely to be a finding that the activity is unauthorised. For example, the parking and maintenance of an ice-cream van within a drive-way has been held to constitute a business use not ancillary to a dwelling-house;[34] there was a detrimental visual effect on the surrounding neighbourhood caused by the presence of the large van. Similarly the use of a small room of a dwelling as a firearms business has been considered a material change of use, owing to the intensity of use and the potentially dangerous equipment involved.[35]

	Planning Permission is not usually needed	Planning Permission is usually needed
USE OF A DWELLING-HOUSE FOR BUSINESS PURPOSES	if the character and use of the building remain essentially residential*	if the character and use of the building do not remain essentially residential*

For example:
- To use part of the house as a bed-sitter or for bed and breakfast accommodation.
- To use a room as your personal office.
- To provide accommodation for a child-minding service or playgroup.
- To use a room for a business such as hairdressing, dressmaking, music teaching, giving tuition or as an insurance or benefit society agency.
- To use a garage to repair cars or store goods connected with a business.

*A change in character or use will probably arise if the answer to any of the following questions is yes:

Will your home no longer be used substantially as a private residence?
Will any part of it no longer be used for private residential purposes?
Will your business result in a marked rise in traffic or people calling?
Will the business involve any activities unusual in a residential area?
Will your business disturb your neighbours at unreasonable hours or be particularly noisy or smelly?

References

1. UCO 1987, Art. 2.
2. Circular 13/87, para. 5.
3. Circular 13/87, para. 24.
4. *Mornford Investments Ltd v Minister of Housing and Local Government* (1970) 21 P&CR 609.
5. *Commercial and Residential Property Development Co. v SSE* [1982] JPL 513.
6. [1985] JPL 783. See also *Thrasyvoulou v SSE* [1988] 3 WLR 1; [1988] 2 PLR 37.
7. [1964] 1 QB 178.
8. [1985] JPL 180.
9. Circular 13/87, para. 27.
10. (1975) 30 P&CR 28.
11. *English Speaking Union v Westminster LBC* (1973) 26 P&CR 575.
12. *Mayflower Cambridge v SSE* (1975) 30 P&CR 28, 32.
13. Circular 13/87, para. 25.
14. UCO 1987, Art. 2.
15. Circular 13/87, para. 5.
16. (1979) 40 P&CR 113; see also *Torbay BC* and *Coughlan* (1986) 1 PAD 269.
17. Circular 13/87, paras. 25–6; see also *Blackpool BC* and *McLoughney* (1988) 3 PAD 312 and *Penwith DC* and *Ellsmore* (1988) 3 PAD 315.
18. *Thanet DC* and *Hurley* (1988) 3 PAD 151.
19. *Barking and Dagenham LBC* and *East London Housing* (1988) 3 PAD 154 and *North Kesteven DC* and *Black* (1988) 3 PAD 415.
20. *Blackpool Borough Council* and *Gregory* (1988) 3 PAD 419.
21. [1988] JPL 793.
22. *Penwith DC* and *Ellsmore* (1988) 3 PAD 315.
23. [1987] JPL 595.
24. [1980] JPL 527; see also [1988] JPL 296.
25. Circular 13/87, para. 27.
26. Circular 13/87, para. 27.
27. T/APP/V0130/A/87/077421/P4; *Woodspring DC* and *Broadway Lodge Ltd.* (1988) 3 PAD 409.
28. *Simmons v Pizzey* (1978) 36 P&CR 36.
29. Circular 13/87, para. 28.
30. Circular 2/86, para. 4.
31. PPG4, para. 17.
32. [1985] JPL 339.
33. [1986] JPL 851; but see *Wigan MBC* and *Nicholson* (1988) 3 PAD 400, where the use of all habitable rooms on the ground floor was held to constitute development.
34. [1988] JPL 202; see also [1978] JPL 789 and [1989] JPL 138.
35. [1989] JPL 54.

9 SOCIAL AND COMMUNITY USES

There are two Use Classes dealing with social and community uses of a non-residential kind:

Class D1: Non-Residential Institutions
Class D2: Assembly and Leisure

Class D1 Non-Residential Institutions

This Use Class includes any use not being a residential use:

(a) for the provision of any medical or health services except the use of premises attached to the residence of the consultant or practitioner,
(b) as a crèche, day nursery or day centre,
(c) for the provision of education,
(d) for the display of works of art (otherwise than for sale or hire),
(e) as a museum,
(f) as a public library or public reading room,
(g) as a public hall or exhibition hall,
(h) for, or in connection with, public worship or religious instruction.

A 'day centre' means premises which are visited during the day for social or recreational purposes or for the purposes of rehabilitation or occupational training at which care is also provided. ('Care' has the same meaning as in Class C1.)

This Class groups together Classes XIII, XV and XVI of the 1972 Order. These were:

Class XIII – Use as a building for public worship or religious instruction or for the social or recreational activities of the religious body using the building.

Class XV – Use (other than residentially) as a health centre, a school treatment centre, a clinic, a crèche, a day nursery or a dispensary, or use as a consulting room or surgery unattached to the residence of the consultant or practitioner.

Class XVI – Use as an art gallery (other than for business purposes), a museum, a public library or reading room, a public hall, or an exhibition hall.

Dispensaries now fall within the terms of the Shops Class. The new class is intended to include day centres, adult training centres and other premises for the provision of non-resident social services as well as non-residential schools and colleges (previously not in any Use Class).[1]

Class D2 Assembly and Leisure

Class D2 includes use as:

(a) a cinema,
(b) a concert hall,
(c) a bingo hall or casino,
(d) a dance hall,
(e) a swimming bath, skating rink, gymnasium or area for other indoor or outdoor sports or recreations, not involving motorised vehicles or firearms.

The assembly and leisure class is based on Classes XVII and XVIII of the 1972 Order. These were:

Class XVII – Use as a theatre, cinema, music hall or concert hall.
Class XVIII – Use as a dance hall, skating rink, swimming bath, Turkish or other vapour or foam bath, or as a gymnasium or sports hall.

This class has been extended to include all indoor and outdoor sports uses except motor sports and sports involving firearms. Theatres have been excluded. This reflects the special protection promoted by the Theatres' Trust Act 1976 and the consequent requirement in the General Development Order for the consultation with the Theatres' Trust before granting planning on land which includes a theatre.[2] There is now said to be an increasing awareness of the importance of London theatre and its vital contribution to London's character and consequently the need to afford it special protection from other potential competing uses.[3]

The circular points out that many outdoor sports require the construction of associated buildings, such as club houses or viewing stands, the erection of which will continue to be subject to specific planning control.[4] Planning permission is of course required for operational development.

There is no Use Class for a social club. Club houses on sports fields should be used for the purposes connected with the sport although ancillary activities such as dances may take place within the primary use for sport itself. A material change of use may be involved where a club house is used for social purposes which are not connected with the sport.[5]

Excluded from this Use Class are amusement arcades and centres which are *sui generis* uses. An 'amusement centre' can cover a wide range of activities some of which are common to bingo halls. Activities which take place in amusement centres can include cash bingo (usually played in bingo clubs), prize bingo, amusement-with-prizes machines (for example, fruit machines) and amusement-only machines (ranging from traditional pin-tables to video games such as 'space invaders').[6] There may be attempts to argue that bingo activities fall within Class D2 (which includes bingo halls) despite the exclusion of amusement centres from the effects of the Order. Such arguments are only likely to succeed where the character of the premises can be said to be as a bingo hall.

References

1. Circular 13/87, paras. 31 and 32.
2. Circular 13/87, para. 31.
3. Whitehall theatre decision: T/APP/X5990/C/84/1054–5/P6.
4. Circular 13/87, para. 31.
5. *Barkmar v SSE* (1984) 271 EG 377.
6. DCPN No. 11, Annex, para. 1.

10 THE GENERAL DEVELOPMENT ORDER

Like the Use Classes Order, the General Development Order is a deregulatory measure so that planning permission is not required for development permitted by that Order. Planning permission may be granted by development order for development specified in the Order, or for development of any class so specified.[1] The current Order is the Town and Country Planning General Development Order 1988.[2] This Order involved a major revision of the 1977 Order which, itself, has been revised on a number of occasions including a revision specifically designed to take into account the 1987 Use Classes Order.[3] Circular 22/88, General Development Order Consolidation, provides a guide to the 1988 Order.

Part 3 of the new General Development Order permits changes of use to take place without planning permission. It replaces Class III of the former General Development Order. Some of these changes were brought into force by the 1987 amendment. Others were foreshadowed in Circular 13/87.[4] Part 4 of the General Development Order deals with temporary uses.

The rights granted by the General Development Order may be restricted by virtue of conditions attached to a planning permission. The rights may be further restricted by a direction under Article 4 of the Order restricting permitted development. There are restrictions on developments involving hazardous substances but these are likely to be amended when the Hazardous Substances Regulations come into force to provide a separate control regime.

The lettering of the classes in the General Development Order is similar to that of the Use Classes Order. To avoid confusion between the two, the classes covered by the General Development Order have been referred to in this chapter as GDO Classes to be differentiated from Use Classes.

Shopping Area Uses

The new General Development Order follows the 1987 revision to the previous General Development Order by permitting development in GDO Class A of Part 3:

> Development consisting of a change of the use of a building to a use falling within Use Class A1 (shops) from a use falling within Use Class

A3 (food and drink) or from a use for the sale, or display for sale, of motor vehicles.

It should be seen that whereas a Food and Drink Class A3 use or a car showroom may change to a shop without the need for planning permission, planning permission is still needed to change a shop to one of those uses.

Similarly under Part 3, there is now permitted GDO Class C which has been added by the new General Development Order:

> Development consisting of a change of use to a use falling within Use Class A2 (financial and professional services) from a use falling within Use Class A3 (food and drink).

GDO Class D is also permitted development related to uses found in shopping areas:

> Development consisting of a change of use of any premises with a display window at ground floor level to a use falling within Use Class A1 (shops) from a use falling within Use Class A2 (financial and professional services).

It can be seen that the Food and Drink Use Class A3 uses may be changed to either shops or financial and professional services without the need for planning permission. Similarly where there is a window display at ground-floor level, financial and professional services uses may be changed to shop uses. However, planning permission is still needed to take premises out of the Shops Use Class or to change the use of financial or professional services to uses falling within the Food and Drink Use Class.

Business Uses

Under Part 3 of the General Development Order, GDO Class B is permitted development which consists of changes of use:

(a) to a use for any purpose falling within Use Class B1 (business) from any use falling within Use Class B2 (general industrial) or B8 (storage and distribution);

(b) to a use for any purpose falling within Use Class B8 (storage and distribution) from any use falling within Use Class B1 (business) or B2 (general industrial).

However development is not permitted by GDO Class B where the change is to or from a use falling within Use Class B8, if the change of use relates to more than 235 m^2 of the floor space in the building.

For general industrial buildings changing to uses falling within the B1 Business Use Class, it should be noted that the restriction of 235 m^2 introduced by the 1987 amendment has been lifted. However, the 235 square metres' restriction still applies to changes of use to and from uses as storage and distribution centres. Moreover there is no permitted development for Use Class B1 uses to be changed to B2 General Industrial uses.

The limitation in size raises the question as to whether warehouse premises over 235 m^2 can be subdivided to form premises under 235 m^2 and then converted to small business units. Subdivision of uses (other than dwelling-houses) falling within Use Classes is permitted.[5] Similarly changes of use of warehouse units under 235 m^2 to business units are permitted under the General Development Order.[6] If the individual units are first used as warehouse units, then such uses should be permitted as the undertaking would not then exceed 235 m^2 at the time of the change. It is an open question, however, whether GDO Class B can be relied upon where the premises are subdivided without being occupied as individual warehouse units before the change of use to business units. It may be argued that as subdivided units, they retain their use rights which can then be relied upon to enable the change to the business use to be made.

Summary of Changes of Use Allowed

The Department have produced a diagrammatic table[7] summarising the changes of use allowed between classes of the Use Classes Order:

By GDO Class	From UCO Class	To UCO Class
A	A3 (food & drink)	A1 (shops)
A	Sale of motor vehicles	A1 (shops)
B(a)	B2 (general industrial)	B1 (business)
B(a)	B8 (storage and distribution)	B1 (business)*
B(b)	B1 (business)	B8 (storage and distribution)*
B(b)	B2 (general industrial)	B8 (storage and distribution)*

* Not permitted where the change of use relates to more than 235 square metres of floor space in the building.

By GDO Class	From UCO Class	To UCO Class
C	A3 (food & drink)	A2 (financial and professional)
D	Premises within A2 (professional and financial) with display window at ground-floor level	A1 (shops)

Special Industrial Uses

Changes may be made to the General Development Order when new proposals are brought forward to deal with special industrial uses.

Multiple Uses

A planning permission may give consent for a number of alternative uses to take place on a site. However, in the past, once the permission was implemented for one use, a further permission was often needed to implement the alternative use. The occupier therefore did not have flexibility concerning the use to which he could put his site once the planning permission was implemented.

GDO Class E of Part 3 now permits changes of uses to alternative uses granted by the same planning permission:

Development consisting of change in the use of any building or other land from a use permitted by a planning permission granted on an application, to another use which that permission would have specifically authorised when it was granted.

However development is not permitted by GDO Class E if:

(a) the application for planning permission was made before 5 December 1988;
(b) it would be carried out more than ten years after the grant of planning permission;
(c) it would result in the breach of any condition, limitation or specification contained in that planning permission in relation to the use in question.

Temporary Uses

The General Development Order permits various temporary uses to occur on land for a limited number of days each year. Under GDO Class B of Part 4, deemed planning permission is granted for the use of any land for any purpose for not more than twenty-eight days in total in any calendar year, and the provision on the land of any moveable structure for the purposes of the permitted use. Only fourteen of the twenty-eight days may be used for:

(a) the holding of a market;
(b) motor car and motor cycle racing including trials of speed, and for practising for these activities;

Development is not permitted under GDO Class B of Part 4 if:

(a) the land in question is a building or is within the curtilage of a building, or
(b) the use of the land is for a caravan site.

The use of land as a caravan site is dealt with under Part 5 of the General Development Order. Part 5 gives deemed permission for the use of land as a caravan site in limited circumstances.

Reversion to Previous Uses

The possibility exists that it may be allowable to revert to a previous use after the General Development Order has been relied upon for a change of use. For example, an industrial undertaker may be able to change the use of his premises to a Class B1 use from a general industrial use under the General Development Order and then change back to a general industrial use. This depends on whether the reasoning of *Cynon Valley v S.O.S.W.*[8] will be found applicable to the new Use Classes and General Development Orders.

References

1. TCPA 1971, s.24.
2. SI 1988, No. 1813, amended by SI 1989, No. 603.
3. SI 1987, No. 765.
4. para, 33.
5. TCPA 1971, s.22(f), as amended.
6. Part 3 Class B. 'Building' in TCPA 1971, s.290, includes any part of a building, suggesting that this provision can be relied upon for different parts of a building. By the Interpretation Act 1978, s.13, this definition is carried

over to the General Development Order in the absence of contrary intention. There is no contrary intention appearing in the definition of 'building' in the General Development Order, but no mention is made of 'building' including part of a building.

7. Circular 22/88, para. 59.
8. [1986] JPL 760. TCPA 1971, s.23(8), and see p. 30, above.

11 COVENANTS AND USE CLASSES

Many restrictive covenants, particularly in leases, define the permitted user by reference to the Use Classes Order. Similarly, rent review clauses in leases may make assumptions as to the permitted user by referring to the Use Classes Order.[1] The problem has now emerged as to how to interpret such provisions in the light of the introduction of the new Use Classes Order.

A provision in an old lease may, for example, restrict the permitted user to Class II of the Use Classes Order uses. The question arises as to whether such a clause should be interpreted as referring to the former Use Class in the 1972 Order or its replacement Classes in the 1987 Order. Obviously the answer is important since what can be permitted under the respective Use Classes is different in each case. This chapter offers suggestions as to how such provisions may be construed but, in each case, the particular provision must be looked at in the light of the whole agreement.

In a document dated prior to 1 June 1987, a restriction referring simply to uses within the 1972 Use Classes Order without further qualification should be interpreted as just referring to the 1972 Order. In such a case there will not be any additional words or clause referring to any replacement or re-enactment thereof or any Order for the time being in force. In such a case the clause is to be interpreted by reference to the circumstances existing at the date of the lease and not to circumstances later.[2]

The 1972 Order was slightly amended on 1 May 1984 by a statutory instrument whose principal effect was to exclude uses where notifiable quantities of hazardous substances were involved. The question arises as to what should a reference to the 1972 Order by itself mean in a lease entered into between 1 May 1984 and 1 June 1987. Usually, the reference should be to the statutory instrument in its amended form. In *Brett v Brett Essex Golf Club*,[3] Slade LJ said:

> ... in many, perhaps the majority of cases where the parties to a written contract have incorporated in it a reference to a statute which has been amended, it may be reasonable to impute to them an intention to refer to the statute in its amended form. However no authority has been cited to us which suggests there is any presumption of construction to that effect.

In that case there were indications that the intention was to refer to the statute in its unamended form; the Court of Appeal followed those pointers. However, where there is no evidence to the contrary, the clause should usually be construed to refer to the statutory instrument in its amended form.

Problems will arise when a document or lease dated prior to 1 June 1987 refers to the Use Classes Order 1972 with additional words to incorporate any replacement or re-enactment of the same Order then in force. In the document, there may also be a general interpretative clause to the effect that references to statutory instruments should refer to the up-to-date provisions. In such a case, it may be argued that the equivalent Use Class of the 1987 Order must be looked at save in the case where it can be fairly said that there is really no equivalent class so that the 1972 Use Class must be relied upon to make sense of the provision.

In the case of the Shops Class, one will normally be justified in taking Class A1 as the equivalent class to Class I. In the case of Classes II and III of the 1972 Order, the question may be asked whether there is an equivalent class in the 1987 Order or whether one may only make sense of the provision by continuing to refer to the text of the 1972 Order. Use as offices in Class II may be interpreted as uses falling within Classes A2 or B1 or both. Similarly a use restricted to Class III may now be interpreted by reference to Class B1 which is considerably wider in scope. Each clause will have to be looked at separately in the context of the whole agreement.

If the Use Classes Order 1987 is to be referred to when drafting new provisions, it will be important to ensure that there is no rider or interpretative clause whereby it can be construed according to a later enactment in times to come. Otherwise there will be no certainty as to how the clause will be interpreted on a subsequent revision to the Use Classes Order.

References

1. *Wolf v Enfield* (1988) 55 P&CR 78.
2. *Compton v Estates Gazette* (1978) 36 P&CR 148; see also R. Bernstein and K. Reynolds, *Handbook of Rent Review*, London, revised ed. 1985, paras. 6–13.
3. [1986] 1 EGLR 154, 157.

INDEX